Also by the same author and available from New English Library:

GUNS OFF CAPE ANNE

H.M.S. KELLY

The Story of Mountbatten's Warship

Kenneth Poolman

NEW ENGLISH LIBRARY/TIMES MIRROR

First published in Great Britain by
William Kimber & Co. Ltd, 1954

First NEL Paperback Edition February 1974
Reprinted August 1980

NEL Books are published by
New English Library Limited from
Barnard's Inn, Holborn,
London EC1N 2JR.
Made and printed in Great Britain by
Hunt Barnard Printing Ltd.,
Aylesbury, Bucks.

450047849

FOREWORD

by Admiral The Earl Mountbatten of Burma,
K.G., P.C., G.C.B., O.M., G.S.C.I., G.C.I.E., G.C.V.O.,
D.S.O.

I WENT to sea as a sixteen-year-old midshipman in the First World War thirty-eight years ago, and since then I have served in some twenty ships. Each ship and her company had their own personality and characteristics, and I have kept very happy memories of each of these ships. But among them all one ship stands out from the others. She was the happiest ship, with the best ship's company I can remember. Most ships have names that have been borne by predecessors over the centuries, but this ship, the *Kelly*, is the only ship ever to have borne this name, and to me she was quite unlike any other ship I have served in.

In 1936 I had just come back after commanding a destroyer in the Mediterranean and was serving at the Admiralty when a friend of mine, a well-known naval constructor called Cole, was designing a new class of destroyers. As we were friends, I used to spend much of my spare time at the Admiralty going through the designs with him and making practical suggestions from my recent experience at sea. And so it came about that I went up to see the leader of this class, the *Kelly*, not very long after her keel had been laid at the Hebburn shipbuilding yard.

In the spring of 1939 I had the unexpected good fortune to be given command of this flotilla leader and of her sister ships that were to form the Fifth Destroyer Flotilla. I watched the *Kelly* being completed at Hebburn, and I was there to receive the new ship's company when they joined to commission the ship.

I was the only captain she ever had, and I knew and loved her from the time of her birth when her keel was laid until the keel was the last thing visible as she sank beneath the waves.

And so I am glad and honoured to have been invited to contribute a Foreword to this book, which has been made possible by drawing upon the memory of so many of her survivors.

I am sure they will all agree with me that although the *Kelly* was a good ship and fought a good war, so did many other destroyers. The tale of the *Kelly* is merely typical of the tale of any of our destroyers during those first two gruelling years of the war. I feel, therefore, that in commemorating the *Kelly* this book is really paying a tribute to all the destroyers that fought so gallantly and well in the days while we still had our backs to the wall.

The *Kelly* was sunk on May 23rd, 1941, in the Battle of Crete. No one left their posts when the end came. She went down with all her guns firing and with all her men at their action stations. We did not leave the *Kelly*, it was she who finally left us; but the spirit of her ship's company lived on, as the spirit of all our other fighting ships did, and it was this spirit that contributed more than anything else to our ultimate victory at sea. This spirit still lives today in the Fleet.

Mountbatten of Burma

CONTENTS

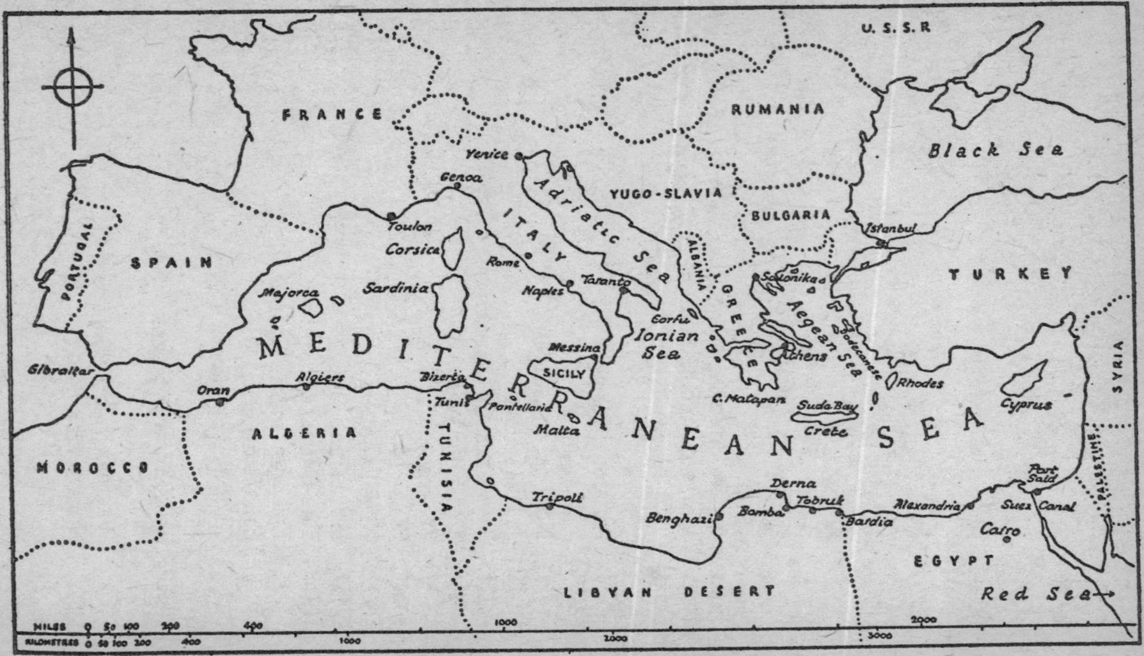

U. S. S. R
FRANCE
RUMANIA
Black Sea
Venice
Genoa
YUGO-SLAVIA
BULGARIA
Adriatic Sea
ITALY
Toulon
Istanbul
PORTUGAL
SPAIN
Corsica
Rome
ALBANIA
TURKEY
Sardinia
Naples
Taranto
Salonika
Mejorca
GREECE
Aegean Sea
Dodecanese
Corfu
Ionian Sea
MEDITERRANEAN SEA
Messina
Athens
SYRIA
SICILY
Rhodes
Gibraltar
Algiers
Bizerta
Oran
Tunis
Pantellaria
C. Matapan
Suda Bay
Cyprus
Malta
Crete
ALGERIA
TUNISIA
MOROCCO
PALESTINE
Port Said
Derna
Tripoli
Tobruk
Alexandria
Suez Canal
Benghazi
Bomba
Bardia
Cairo
EGYPT
LIBYAN DESERT
Red Sea
MILES 0 50 100 200 400 1000 2000
KILOMETRES 0 50 100 200 400 1000 2000 3000

AUTHOR'S PREFACE

I FIRST wanted to write this story some ten years ago. As a completely undistinguished 'hostilities only' able seaman, I received a draft chit to the destroyer *Kimberley*, a survivor of Lord Mountbatten's famous Fighting Fifth Flotilla. Aboard *Kimberley* I heard from some of the real sailors stories of the old flotilla, and particularly of its leader, the *Kelly*.

It was not until some time later that I realised how the story of one ship might be made to tell a larger tale. For the *Kelly*'s war, interesting as it is in itself, reflects a nation's struggle in those first two dark years of endurance. In particular, this one ship reflects the stubborn, gallant fight put up by the men of the Royal Navy, always with a fierce, fighting spirit and a grin for the irony of it all – the spirit born out by the immortal words:

'Shouldn't have joined if I can't take a joke.'

So I offer this story now, in all humility, as one man's

view of a destroyer in wartime – a brief record of the doings of a group of personalities, and of the background against which they did what they did, both comic and serious.

Not the least among these personalities is the *Kelly* herself, whose history I have tried to follow right from the time when she was nothing but a gleam in her architect's eye.

For those not familiar with naval slang and general terminology I have added a short glossary.

I have received help from many sources in the preparation of this book. First and foremost are the men of the *Kelly* themselves, of whom so many have given me their time and invaluable help. It would be impossible to name them all here and invidious to mention individuals.

I owe a great debt of gratitude to Mr Holmes of the department of the Chief of Naval Information at the Admiralty. I am also grateful to the B.B.C. for permission to incorporate in the book material used previously in a feaure programme called 'Destroyer'. Messrs R. & W. Hawthorn, Leslie & Co. Ltd, the builders of *Kelly* and of so many other splendid ships, have been kindness itself. Indeed, without their help my job would have been impossible. To my wife I owe a great debt for interpreting my scrawl so efficiently and patiently.

I wish to express my thanks to Mr Charles Causley for permission to quote from his book *Farewell, Aggie Weston's*, published by the Hand and Flower Press; to Messrs Jarrolds Ltd for the extracts from the late Ray Murphy's book *Last Viceroy*; to the *Daily Mirror* for quotations from an article published on December 7th, 1940; to the Victoria Music Publishing Co. Ltd for the verse from 'Me and My Dog' by Vivian Ellis; and to Major Stephen Foot, D.S.O., and Moral Re-Armament, London, for permission to quote from the pamphlet *Wisdom from the Sea*.

KENNETH POOLMAN

CHAPTER I

No. 615

On the quayside at Hawthorn Leslie's shipbuilding yard, Hebburn-on-Tyne, stood three lines of men in navy blue. They stood at ease, with their kitbags and hammocks piled up around them, staring at the ship that lay alongside.

She was new, brand-new. Her brasswork was bright, and she was painted in pale grey Mediterranean colours. Brightest of all were the letters of her name, up in bold brass over the quarterdeck. 'Kelly', they read.

'Kelly,' said Second Class Stoker Gordon Rogers to himself, 'Kelly.' It didn't sound like an Isle of Man boat any more, now that he could see what went with the name. He turned his head and looked at the raking funnel, the long torpedo-tubes, the hunched, silent bulk of the guns, the tearaway, flaring bow and sharp stem.

She looked smaller than he had expected – ships always do – and more *mechanical*. But she was beautiful. Because her role demanded swiftness as well as power, her lines were sweet and slender, her silhouette streamlined, rakish and low. You could see all that at a glance. And there wasn't an inch of space to spare. Everything fitted and was designed to function within its own tight arc of action, without fuss and without any trimmings. After all, this wasn't a yacht – this was a Fleet destroyer.

He looked at the funnel, which rose up in front of him a few yards away – a big exhaust pipe from the boilers, but graceful for all that, with a tilt that gave a dashing, cocky look to the whole ship. At the other end of the exhaust pipe were the boilers, and they would be his concern. Number one boiler-room, down there under the break of the fo'c'sle, would be his place of business from now on.

It was a big jump from a tobacconist's shop in Liverpool. For a moment he wished himself back in Sefton Park, behind the counter. As he looked at the cold, harsh outline of his new home he wondered how he would get on.

If the ship was new, so was he, and so were many others in the new ship's company. Rogers was fresh from a stone frigate and this was his first ship. A new matelot, a new ship. Where would she carry him? What would she teach him? And how would he learn it? How would he make out?

From the quarterdeck the Captain examined his ship's company. A raw enough bunch, on the whole, he thought. It wouldn't be easy for them.

It wouldn't be easy for him, either. In many ways he, too, was raw. You may be an experienced, brilliant officer, singled out by Their Lordships for the command of a crack new flotilla of destroyers embodying the very latest in design. You may be a man of dash and energy and technical virtuosity, but the fact remains that you haven't been on the bridge of a destroyer for a long time. Your ship-handling can get rusty after three years in a desk job at the Admiralty. And that was only one ship. Now it was a whole flotilla.

No, it would not be easy for any of them. The Captain stood there, tall and outwardly calm, wondering how they would all shape up as a team.

'Ship's company, 'SHUN! Into file, left TURN. Front rank, right wheel, quick MARCH!'

The first man stepped on to the wooden brow that linked ship with shore across the strip of oily water and went inboard. The future was upon them.

The future. But what of the past? A ship is not built in a day, and this ship's story had started many months before....

German and Japanese observers at the Royal Naval Coronation Review of 1937 had ample justification for indulging in complacency. The long lines of British ships, impressive enough to the layman's eye, did not stand up so well to expert scrutiny, and the senior officers of the *Graf Spee* and the *Asigara* would certainly miss nothing.

To begin with, there were far too many old units in the Review Fleet. Of the eleven battleships present at Spithead none could be described as modern; and the two strongest ships, *Nelson* and *Rodney*, had been reduced in size and gunpower from their original design by treaty regulations. Fourteen cruisers took part in the Review. Of these only four – *Southampton* and *Newcastle* (launched in 1936), *Leander* (1931) and *Galatea* (1934) – were of recent design.

Of the force of fifty destroyers present many were fine ships, but nearly half of the total number had been completed either during or shortly after the First World War. In fact, thirteen of them were of the old Admiralty 'V' and 'W' design, built under the Emergency War Programme of 1918. Their armament of four-inch guns and six triple torpedo-tubes was not up to modern standards.

But although the age of so many of its ships gave serious cause for concern, a far greater weakness of the Royal

Navy at that time lay in lack of numbers and, in particular, in the serious shortage of cruisers and destroyers. With the international situation as volatile as it was, a world war would find Great Britain with insufficient ships to guard her trade routes and overseas commitments and at the same time meet all the normal Fleet requirements. The age of the old 'Vs' and 'Ws' mattered less than the fact that far too many of their sister-ships had been sent to the breakers after the First World War – ships that would have been worth their weight in gold now.

In the event of a war with Germany the protection of ships carrying vital imports and exports to and from the British Isles would be the Navy's main task. And there were not enough ships to go round. The presence of a German pocket battleship at the Naval Review was in itself a reminder of a form of naval warfare familiar to the German Navy – that of long-range commerce raiding by heavy units – which we could certainly expect if war broke out again. Add to this the possibility of intensive U-boat warfare, and the crying necessity for large numbers of powerful convoy escorts and anti-submarine vessels became plain. The Italian Fleet, too, might well represent a serious threat to Britain's control of the seas. Although the spirit and efficiency of Italian sailors were doubtful quantities, Mussolini was known to possess a large fleet of modern ships, including numerous destroyers.

However, the situation was not as black as it appeared on the surface. Those who saw only lack of preparation in Britain's fighting forces and 'appeasement' in her foreign policy were misreading the signs. Beside her sincere efforts for peace in Europe, Britain was playing for time, time to build a new military machine, to give her forces the modern weapons and equipment necessary to face the threat of war. Behind the scenes she went to work. In particular the Royal Air Force was to be expanded. Orders were placed for the Spitfires and Hurricanes that were to give the Luftwaffe lessons their 'manoeuvres' against women and children in Spain had not taught them.

The Navy, too, was expanding. The Emergency Programme of Naval Construction for 1937 was the biggest since the First World War. Additions to all branches of the Fleet were planned.

The 1935 Estimates had already provided for the building of sixteen new destroyers. These were the ships of the 'Tribal' class. The Tribals were all in an advanced stage of building and were expected to be launched during the year, to be finally completed in 1938. They were splendid ships, carrying an armament that leaned heavily upon gunpower. A very heavy broadside of eight twin-mounted 4·7-inch guns was to be carried, although this was to be done at the expense of torpedo armament, of which only one set of quadruple tubes would be fitted. They were 'destroyers' in the full sense of the word, able to outfight anything in the flotillas of foreign navies, including the new German destroyers. Their value as convoy escorts could be imagined, though it would be unlikely that many of them could be spared for that job.

Now, close on the heels of the Tribals, came a new class of destroyer, of improved design and with a big difference in the distribution of armament. The contract for the first two ships of this class, both flotilla leaders, went to the famous Tyneside firm of Messrs R. & W. Hawthorn, Leslie and Co. Ltd.

The firm of Hawthorn Leslie had a long, proud record. Only twelve years after the Battle of Trafalgar Robert Hawthorn started his Steam Engine Works at Forth Banks, Newcastle-upon-Tyne, with four employees. The country was then in the grip of the Industrial Revolution, and the great advances in engineering that the men of the north-east had done so much to bring about were being extended to shipbuilding. Three years after Robert Hawthorn had started his Engine Works he began to build marine engines. The first of these was a little seven-horse-power engine for a Tyne packet. Seven horse-power had become 150, when, in 1862, the St Peter's works received its first machinery order from the British Government for the engines of a new gun-boat.

Meanwhile, ships were being built in large numbers all along the banks of the Tyne. One of the most flourishing yards was that of Andrew Leslie at Hebburn. When Andrew Leslie first came to Hebburn in 1853 green fields and farmlands stretched down to the river. The following year fields had given place to slipways, and shady trees to gaunt cranes. He built his first ship that year, just in time for her to be chartered by the Government and to serve in the Crimean War. The firm soon gained an outstanding reputation for first-class workmanship. During the next twenty-two years they constructed 265 ships.

Leslie used Hawthorn's engines to power his ships, and in 1885 the two firms were amalgamated under the name they bear today. The new century brought in new trends in naval construction. One of these was the torpedo-boat, and the firm specialised in this new development from the very beginning. In 1899 they had built H.M.S. *Viper,* the first vessel (other than the experimental *Turbinia*) to be fitted with turbines, which reached a speed of thirty-seven knots, proving herself the fastest vessel of her period. After the torpedo-boat came its countermeasure, the torpedo-boat destroyer. Hawthorn Leslie remained the leaders in the construction of these fast, graceful craft, and in the First World War over a score of fine destroyers came off their slipways. One of these, the *Marksman,* built in 1915, was one of the first of a new variation – the flotilla leader. This type of ship, as her name implies, was specially equipped to carry the senior officer of the flotilla, Captain (D), and his staff, and had naturally to be the very last word in design and construction.

This, then, was the family tree of the two new 'leaders' ordered from the Hebburn yard. On the firm's books they were designated 'No. 614' and 'No. 615'. No. 614 had been contracted for in 1936 and was the senior ship of the two by a few months.

On April 2nd, 1937, when the first two Tribals, *Afridi* and *Cossack,* were still two months away from launching, the contract was signed for the second ship, No. 615. Then followed all the usual preliminaries to the actual commencement of work upon a ship. The contract drawings, showing the general lay-out and arrangement of the ship, were put into the hands of the builders, who, after due consultation and discussion with the Admiralty, signed them. From these general drawings the working drawings were prepared, and the various parts of the ship's hull drawn full-size in chalk on the blackboard-like floor of the mould loft. From these chalk outlines the wooden moulds were made and taken to the shops, where they were used to shape the actual parts of the new hull. By that time preparations were in hand in the building berth. Keel blocks were laid down the centre of the crane-lined slope, from the point where, in two years time, the christening bottle would be swung against tall grey bows, down to the edge of the black river.

On August 26th the keel of No. 615 was laid and work begun. Shortly afterwards the Director, Naval Construction, affirmed to the Controller of the Navy that

> In accordance with your instructions, work is proceeding on the design of a flotilla leader having the following characteristics: Armament, six 4.7-inch guns, one 2-pdr. pom-pom, two 0.5-inch machine-guns, two 21-inch quintuple torpedo-tubes. Speed 32 knots.

She was new, no doubt about that. Considered all round, her armament was a distinct advance upon that of the Tribals. The loss of one twin 4.7 would be more than made up for by the increase in torpedo-power – two quintuple tubes instead of one quadruple. Of course, some difference in function was also intended. The increase in torpedo armament seemed to indicate that the newer ships were more particularly intended for close co-operation with the Fleet.

But her armament was by no means her only new and outstanding feature. To begin with, she was to have a lower, smaller silhouette than previous destroyers, with only one low, fairly squat funnel. There were also radical improvements in her engine-room design. She was to have two boilers instead of three, but the reduction in boilers meant no loss of power. Her machinery was designed to develop a total of 40,000 shaft horse-power and was to be based upon swin-screw, single-reduction geared turbines of the Parsons type. An astern turbine was to be incorporated in each low-power turbine and provision made in the high-power turbines to ensure a high degree of efficiency over a wide range of cruising powers.

One of the most novel features in the design of No. 615 was in the construction of her hull. Previous destroyers had been built on what is known as the 'transverse system'. The framework of a warship's hull is based on an arrangement of intersecting girders. These are disposed so that some run fore-and-aft, parallel to the keel of the ship, and are called either 'longitudinals' (those at the bottom of the ship's hull) or 'stringers' (those at the sides of the hull), while others, called 'frames', are set transversely or athwart-ships. In the old system the frames were in the majority, the longitudinals and stringers being, though fewer, of necessity 'deeper', i.e. wider in section, than the frames. In the new system the order was reversed. The longitudinals and stringers were greatly increased, and the frames decreased in number, while this time the frames were made deeper. This was called the 'longitudinal system'. The idea, which was an adaptation of the Isherwood system of design previously used in the construction of tankers, was intended to provide a stiffer hull against the hard knocks of sea-time and possible enemy action – an important consideration in the construction of a destroyer, which is in the front line of naval warfare and spends nearly all her life at sea.

There were to be innovations, too, in living conditions – a general improvement in the living quarters of the ship's company. This affected particularly the crew space for'ard. The messdecks would be very much more spacious than in previous destroyers and there were to be bathrooms attached. Various 'buzzes' which went round barracks to the effect that the new Navy was to have bunks after the American style, with washing (dhobeying) and even ice-cream machines, not to mention cafeteria messing, were to be proved unfounded – in this ship, at any rate. The ship's company of No. 615 would still be slinging their hammocks on the messdecks. There would still be the rush to grab a cushy billet near a steam-pipe, where a matelot could hang his boots and keep his matches and early morning fag at the ready. There would still be cooks of the mess, and they would still have to scrub out for rounds and draw and prepare the food for the mess. There would still be a space for the 'scran-bag'; and dhobeying would still be done in a bucket, using pusser's soap and super-hot water from the for'ard boiler-room (if you had an oppo down there).

But *bathrooms,* and with *green tiles*! It is recorded that when the first members of the new ship's company feasted their depot-dulled eyes on all this luxury there were comparisons, not unfavourable, with the Ritz, the Savoy, the Waldorf Astoria in Yankeeland, and even with Aggie Weston's in Chatham. It is also to be had on good authority that the petty officers immediately demanded a blue room. In fact, to many minds she was a bit too good to be true; as the leading seaman wrote in his first letter home from the ship, 'She's just like a first-class yacht all ready for a cruise.'

This new ship, then, her sister, No. 614, and the other ships of her class to be built, were to help fill the gap in British destroyer strength. They, and all the ships planned as part of the new building programme, formed part of an attempt to make up for the idle years of British naval enterprise. But, welcome as they would be to a depleted Fleet, they represented only a fraction of the numbers that would be needed to fight a war against Germany. With powerful commerce-raiders as well as submarines to face and overcome, the Fleet would have to be increased many times over before it could be called adequate. And there might not be time.

The threat from German capital ships operating against our ocean trade routes would almost certainly be the first to be put into action in war. Capital ships could only be stopped by capital ships – fast battleships, battle-cruisers or aircraft-carriers operating torpedo-planes. But we had no fast battleships, although several were building, and only three battle-cruisers, while torpedo-planes could easily be prevented by bad weather from operating at all. In any case our aircraft-carrier strength was still inadequate, and scouting patrols as well as anti-submarine activity could be expected to make urgent claims upon its services.

The second serious threat would come from U-boat warfare. Again, submarines could only be sunk by fast anti-submarine craft, patrolling ceaselessly in large numbers, or by aircraft (although little was then known of the latter method). Thirdly, convoys would need large numbers of escorting warships.

From all these considerations it could be seen that heavy demands would be made upon the destroyers, the traditional maids-of-all-work.

There would still not be anywhere near enough to go round. The Fleet would have first call on the new destroyers, with their heavy torpedo armament, and upon the most powerful units in the existing flotillas. The convoys would have to make do, in the main, with the older ships until new escorts could be built. In fact these older vessels – and that meant mainly the old 'V' and 'W' destroyers – were to prove themselves well up to the job.

But there were not enough of them. If war broke out within the next two years the navy would still be compelled to operate for a long time on a shoe-string, and it would be the cold-shouldered peacetime navy, ships and men, that would have to stand the first shock. In that event the new destroyers could look forward to a gruelling war.

A shoe-string navy, then; but without the Emergency Programme not even a shoe-string.

Work on the new ships was pressed forward as speedily as possible without neglecting quality. At Hebburn, throughout months of painstaking craftsmanship and labour, the skeleton of No. 615 slowly grew. From the narrow backbone of her keel the ribs of her frames arose; the stem was fitted, stern and propeller-shaft brackets put in. Then, slowly, the first framework was clothed with plates. She was in that stage now when she looked less like a new ship than an old hulk waiting to be scrapped, for the weather had covered her plating with a dew of rust. The metal shell vibrated ceaselessly with the angry chatter of riveting and the clangour of metal on metal. The tall cranes inclined stiffly over the steel carcase, lowering beams and bulkheads and plating into position.

At the same time parallel efforts were being made on the building of the other seven ships of her future flotilla in shipyards all over the country. Each firm concerned with the building of the 'Js' and 'Ks', as the first sixteen ships were to be called, was entrusted with the construction of two vessels, one 'J' class and one 'K'. Hawthorn Leslie's were building the leaders of both flotillas, and the firm strove hard to make them the finest products the yard had ever turned out. No. 615, in particular, was the apple of her builder's eye. She might have been built with silver rivets.

Meanwhile, the clouds grew gradually darker over Europe, and war seemed day by day more imminent.

As 1937 passed into 1938 the threat increased. In March

the Nazis bullied a frightened Austria into accepting German domination, and Nazi troops crossed the frontier. The British Government, beyond observing 'that what has passed cannot fail to have prejudiced the hope of His Majesty's Government of removing misunderstandings between nations and promoting international co-operation', remained passive, though uneasy, spectators of the tragedy. Although Mr Chamberlain believed, whatever the state of British military preparedness, in the ideal of peace in Europe as the first and all-important object of our foreign policy, nevertheless behind the British attitude to Hitler's ominous encroachments on European freedom was the demoralising thought that the country was not yet ready to challenge force with force. In the breathing space our yards and factories worked steadily on. Slowly the fighters came off the assembly-lines, the weapons of war multiplied.

When the second big crisis came, in September, the ships of the shoe-string navy were still only half built in the yards. Throughout the year German agitation against Czechoslovakia had been growing in intensity, ostensibly on behalf of the 'persecuted' German minorities in that country. In September the mounting campaign of propaganda reached its height. The German army was poised on the Czech frontier and seemed about to strike. At that point Mr Chamberlain made two trips to Germany to attempt to negotiate with the Fuehrer for a reasonable settlement of the Sudeten question, but so unsatisfactory were Hitler's replies to his proposals and so extravagant his counter-proposals that, when the Prime Minister returned from the Godesberg conference on September 24th, war seemed inevitable. The Navy was mobilised, and the organisation of civil-defence precautions begun as the situation deteriorated rapidly. But on September 29th two dictators and two prime ministers met in Munich. Their discussions produced a new and considerably modified statement of German demands upon Czechoslovakia. These were accepted at once by the Czech Government and the world breathed again. It was 'peace in our time'.

But Britain had learnt her lesson: that her efforts for peace must be backed by force. In the factories and shipyards work on the tools of freedom went steadily on. And in the recruiting offices....

'So you want to join the Navy, son?'

'Yes, sir.'

'How old are you?'

'Twenty-four, sir.'

'What do you want to go as?'

'Well, sir, I know morse code and I thought I'd like to go as a signals bloke.'

'Well, you can't lad, the age limit is twenty-three for the communications branch. But you can go as a stoker.'

'Yes; all right, sir. I'll go as a stoker.'

'Right. Come over here and I'll test your eyes.'

Gordon Rogers from Liverpool was joining the Navy. He looked out of the window at the cold February day. It wasn't too late – he hadn't signed anything yet.

'Come on then, put this card over your right eye and read the bottom line.'

'A E B G D F....'

He passed, but his fellow-volunteer had a bit of trouble.

'Do you think I need glasses, sir?'

'Glasses? You need a bloody white stick, son. Sorry, and mind the step as you go out.'

Rogers was all alone now – an oddity, an eccentric, who'd had the silly idea that he wanted to join the Navy. It still wasn't too late....

'Changed your mind, son?'

'No, sir.'

'Good, because you've got perfect eyesight, laddie. Look, the age limit for a signalman is twenty-three. Now, *how* old did you say you were?'

He loves me, he loves me not, he loves me . . . Two can play at that game, Admiral.

'Twenty-four.'

'Okay, if that's the way you want it, a stoker it is.'

Yes, this was the way he wanted it. Any 'Scouse' has briny whiskers, and Rogers already had three brothers serving in the Navy. He had tried various jobs. For a time he had painted houses until he had fallen once too often off the ladder. Then he tried his hand a keeping a little tobacconist's-cum-newsagent's business. But he was no shopkeeper. He was young, the blood was hot in his veins, and somehow, after the way of the English, a few grains of salt had got mixed up with it. The sea was after him. After a while he found he just couldn't resist her. So here he was, bewitched and betrothed, launched upon a new life.

And on October 25th, 1938, a little less than a month after the Munich agreement, another launching took place. It was No. 615.

She was to be named *Kelly,* after Admiral of the Fleet Sir John Kelly, whose daughter, Miss Antonia Kelly, spoke the auspicious words: 'I name this ship *Kelly.* May God guide her and guard and keep all who sail in her,' and broke the crystal bottle against the bows.

Thus, with a splash of champagne and a prayer, she was christened and the brittle hull slid down stern first into the black Tyne, to be towed along the river to the Engine Works and tied up alongside her sister destroyer, the *Jervis.* She was a thing of beauty already – a slim, graceful shape with the flare of speed at her bows and a rakish tilt to her superstructure. They lay in the stream, two aristocrats, sprung from a great and illustrious family. 'No. 615' was no more. She had a name now. But she had to be given a heart, a 40,000-horse-power heart.

With the fitting of her machinery, the first man of her future ship's company came up to Hebburn, and a brass hat was seen amongst the dockyard caps and bowlers. It belonged to Commander (E) M. G. Evans, who was to be the Chief Engineer of *Kelly*, with the duty of Flotilla Engineer as well. Commander Evans had come north to supervise the fitting of engines and boilers, and in general to keep an eye on anything and everything that effected his own department.

The naval architect principally concerned with the design of *Kelly*, as he had been, in fact, with all destroyers built for the Navy since 1934, was Mr A. P. Cole. To him went the lion's share of the credit for the innovations in design embodied in this, his latest and finest work. Among the valuable assistance he received in the furtherance of his ideas was the essentially practical co-operation of an officer who had actually returned from commanding a destroyer in the Mediterranean the year before *Kelly*'s keel was laid, Captain Lord Louis Mountbatten.

Mountbatten's star as a sailor was bright and in the ascendant. A cousin to the King, he was himself the son of a great sailor.

Admiral of the Fleet the Marquess of Milford Haven had been a great, and in the end a tragic, figure in the long line of illustrious British admirals. As First Sea Lord, he had been largely responsible for bringing the British Fleet into a state of readiness for the outbreak of war with Germany in 1914, and had forestalled German designs at sea by personally giving the order which kept the Home Fleet mobilised on the very eve of war. But in spite of his high qualities as leader and patriot, Prince Louis of Battenberg, as he then was, was swept from office by the great wave of anti-German hysteria which found in his own German family connections such an easy scapegoat.

His son, too, had reason on his own behalf to be wary of public opinion. Press and public had known him as a social figure, the descendant of royalty, the dashing A.D.C. to the Prince of Wales, the handsome husband of beautiful heiress Edwina Ashley. Too often he was quoted as the lion of cocktail parties, too little as the hardworking sailor he really was.

He began his active service in the right school. Every young midshipman in the Fleet would have given a year's pay for the chance to serve under Admiral Beatty, whose drive and daring must have found a direct reflection in the heart of Midshipman Mountbatten. After service in the *Lion* and *Queen Elizabeth,* both flagships, he became First Lieutenant of an escort vessel.

As a First Lieutenant he was outstanding and, in particular, was recommended for his understanding of the men in his charge. His was not the strict class-consciousness, the hidebound reserve of so many regular officers. From his natural humanity and his wide interests in people, places and things in the modern world, Mountbatten had begun to develop the common touch. He liked people and showed it. More important, he respected them, high or low, and proved it by his obvious interest in their doings and his knowledge of their problems. He preached humanity and decency in human relations and practised what he preached. Those who had these qualities in them invariably returned the compliment. Among these were all the men of the lower deck who ever served under him.

When it came his turn to specialise, Mountbatten chose the wireless-telegraphy branch, and in this department he excelled himself. On the Long Signals Course at Portsmouth he passed out top and proceeded to occupy various positions as a wireless officer both ashore and afloat. As an instructor he was unsurpassed. Again, because he understood men he had the gift of putting over his expert knowledge of a difficult technical subject easily and attractively. Here his flair for the mechanical helped him, and he would often arrange some interesting gadget to illustrate a lesson. In various periods of service with the Mediterranean Fleet he raised the standards of wireless telegraphy to a level unknown before. He compiled his own wireless manual for the use of the Fleet, and true to his concern for the welfare of his branch, he helped to raise the status and pay of naval telegraphists.

Mountbatten had been Flotilla Signals Officer with a destroyer flotilla, and had already seen much service in destroyers when he was given command, first of the destroyer *Daring,* and later of the 'V' and 'W' class *Wishart.*

So when he relinquished command of the *Wishart* to take up an appointment at the Admiralty he came back to London as an old destroyer man with a keen professional interest in the small ships and many ideas for their improvement, gleaned from practical experience on the bridge.

At the Admiralty he and Cole discussed these ideas in the light of the new destroyers then building. Between them, architect and sailor evolved an entirely new type of bridge, comprising many original features. Not least among these new fittings was a special device invented by Captain Mountbatten himself, which would enable ships to keep station upon each other automatically when the officer of the watch might be more urgently occupied, as at the height of an engagement at sea.

Captain Mountbatten had often appeared at Hebburn to watch the gradual growth of the fighting ship that he had helped to bring into being, it was a fitting climax to his interest in the new ship when he was, in the spring of 1939, nominated for the command of H.M.S. *Kelly* and of the other seven ships which were to form the Fifth Destroyer Flotilla: *Kingston, Kipling, Kimberley, Kelvin, Kashmir, Khartoum* and *Kandahar.*

Captain Mountbatten immediately went to Hebburn and stood by the *Kelly,* now nearing completion. During that uneasy summer of 1939, he went round visiting each of the other seven ships and had all their commanding officers to stay with him for a weekend so that they could discuss future policy for training the flotilla. This was followed by a meeting between Captain (D) and his engineer officers, after which they all went on a short course under Rear-Admiral (E) Dight at Haslar so that they could all learn together exactly how quickly the new ships could accelerate and produce the best possible engine-room result.

Meanwhile more navy blue began to appear in the chaos of cranes, wires and red lead. Petty Officer Telegraphist Primrose came up to supervise the installing of the wireless equipment. What he saw impressed him. He found that the dockyard had matters in his department well in hand, and his role was confined to keeping a watchful eye on the fitting of the new gear.

Already it was becoming obvious that *Kelly* was something special. Commander Evans could see from the state of affairs in the engine-room department that the flotilla leader was a good 'un long before her trials started, and Petty Officer Primrose observed, as did anyone with half an eye for ships, that *Kelly* was a 'a tiddley job'. The builders were obviously sparing nothing to make her their pride and joy. Primrose found that the wireless office was much larger than the one in which he had worked in his last ship, another destroyer, and that the new design included a great deal of centralisation, making for greater simplicity and efficiency in the running of the department. The fire-control transmitter had been fitted in the main wireless office instead of in a separate one. That was a new idea, and so was the frequency-measuring equipment, which could be used to set the transmitter and receiver to any frequency without having to waste time searching for it. Primrose was on his own for a while, then in June two telegraphists arrived from barracks and he immediately gave them the job of rigging aerials.

CHAPTER II

A DRAFT CHIT

PETTY OFFICER WRITER BOB KNIGHT wondered what to expect of the new ship.

A naval writer's lot is not always a happy one. Nelson himself once said, 'I hate your pen and ink men'; and it is easy to see how prejudice against the white-collar workers of the Navy can exist. Ashore, the flat 'at calls the homburg names. Afloat, the seaman looks sideways upon the man who is always on the right side of the table at Defaulters, who hobnobs with the officers, who helps to see you off at pay-day, the pampered one who sits warming his bottom on a chair in the ship's office while you are mucking about with wires and fenders or shivering on a wet fo'c'sle. It's all right for some.

So the writer is always a bit of a pariah on the mess-decks. Nobody likes the writer.

Bob Knight was not feeling too happy now as he stood on the quayside. Betwixt and between, neither of the old ship nor the new, he was in the limbo of the draft. This no-man's-land begins just outside the barrack gates, where the draft lorry starts its journey to the station. The draftee stares out over the tailboard at a lost heaven that he had once looked on, blind fool, as something like a jail, with himself as its prisoner. Then comes the long wretchedness of transportation, and journey's end with his first sight of the unfamiliar silhouette alongside the jetty. He is still unsettled, vaguely miserable. It is the misery of the exile, and sailors know it well.

But for Knight, at any rate, the silhouette of *Kelly* was not as unfriendly as it might have been. To begin with, he was highly delighted to have been picked to serve aboard a flotilla leader which, so the buzz ran, was going to the Mediterranean station.

Visions of that glittering, ancient sea came into his mind. He thought of Gib. and the Spanish dancers, their dark eyes deep with the reflection of the exotic country across the water. Then tawny Africa, gleaming like a mirage over to starboard, with the bows dipping through azure water, heading for the burning zenith of the Delta, white-hot Cairo and Alexandria, sprawled like a leopard in the fierce light – the familiar pavements of Ramleh Square, the old Fleet Club and the tramride out to Stanley Bay with its perverse extremes of burning sand and cool, clear sea.

He thought of Malta, the matelot's Riviera – Malta, green in winter like a leaf on a blue lake, in summer brown as a biscuit in the baking heat. He swam in St Paul's Bay, the water blue out in the deeps and pale emerald in the shallows, with the foam white like coconut milk. He drained a long, cool drink in that little hotel at Birzebbuga and lazed on the balcony there, watching the bright boats in the bay. He strolled down narrow, noisy Kingsway on a cool evening, navigating slowly the deep, restless murmur of the crowd, stopping for a fling at Tombola or a beer in a quiet bar on the shadowed side of the street. He watched the sun setting over the sea beyond yellow rocks and water shot with purple light. From a rooftop in Floriana he looked across the darkened water – dim gangway lights, the distant muffled warble of a bosun's call, and the lamps of small boats flitting from shore to shore like fireflies.

He saw the blue tongue of the Grand Harbour, with the bright-painted dghaisas gliding from Custom's House Steps across the sunlight to St Angelo, over the smooth water that reflected the tall pile of palaces and ancient churches towering into the hot sky like wedding cakes in honey-coloured stone. Yes, a jewel, Valetta, set amidst pearls and ivory. In his mind's eye he saw the *Kelly* lying in Grand Harbour, with her white awnings spread and her brasswork gleaming.

The visions faded and his real eye took in the *Kelly* lying alongside Hawthorn Leslie's yard at Hebburn-on-Tyne, just across the oily water from cold Northumberland. Nevertheless she was a sight worth seeing. He had never seen such a smart, spick-and-span-looking ship before. The colour of her paintwork was glossy light-grey enamel, her decks were spotless, and her brasswork shone like a new penny.

So the advance party arrived, like new settlers in a virgin land. They found themselves thrown into the midst of Trials.

There had been numerous preliminary trials and inspections throughout May, with the ship still lying alongside the jetty. Then, on Friday, June 2nd, smoke was seen drifting upwards from the black-topped funnel. *Kelly*, was 'flashed up'; she had steam on her boilers for the first time. That month saw a long succession of preliminary equipment trials – trials of the refrigerating machinery, the earliest tests of the torpedo equipment. The wireless gear was inspected and tested and the sets tuned, and *Kelly* had her first trials of anchors and capstan. By the beginning of July she was ready for a more important stage of examination. The builders sent a communication to the Admiralty headed 'Contract Shipbuilders' Certificates of the Satisfactory Condition of H.M.S. *Kelly* while away from their Premises for the Purpose of Trials, etc.' In this they certified:

> . . . that the vessel is in a proper condition to undertake these Trials, and that the state of completion of the vessel as regards general Structural Condition, Bulkheads, Decks and Flats, W.T. Doors and Scuttles in connection therewith, W.T. Ports on Side, Side Scuttles, Battening down and other arrangements for the exclusion of water from the interior of the vessel, Boats, Boatlifting Appliances and Stowage of Boats, etc., is satisfactory. . . .
>
> Also that the Supports to Guns and the Hull Fittings in connection with the Guns, Steering Gear and its controlling apparatus, etc., Anchor and Capstan Gear, have, so far as is practicable prior to the vessel being under way, been tested in accordance with the Specification . . .
>
> Also that the Wireless Telegraphy Installation, Cabin, Messing, and Berthing accommodation, including Cooking and Baking Apparatus, Pumping, Lighting and Ventilating arrangements, Fire Service, Navigational Fittings . . . are in all respects in a sufficiently satisfactory condition for the purpose of Naval requirements during these Trials.

In other words, *Kelly* was ready to show her paces, and her builders were ready and eager to show her off before the exacting eyes of the Admiral Superintendent Contract Built Ships.

The preliminary sea trials were divided into several sections. They began with the adjustment of the ship's compasses and the inspection of her gyro-compass equipment. These were followed by anchor trials, which involved the testing of brakes and the heaving in of each anchor at the proper speed. The ship then steamed for an hour at full power, and for the first time her 40,000-horsepower was given its head. Steering trials, log trials, trials of the direction-finding equipment and of the echo-sounding gear followed in quick succession. That was the programme for Tuesday, July 4th. At seven-thirty on the morning of the following Thursday *Kelly* went through her consumption trials. She carried out manœuvering trials on one boiler only and her first experience of the measured mile off St Abbs. Saturday brought her full-power trials – several hours steaming at full power, including a series of four runs on the measured mile and full-power manoeuvering, both ahead and astern, with a final session of steering trials. The preliminary sea-trial programme was finally rounded off on the following Monday with the performance of turning trials.

And still they went on. After the sea trials there was a final inspection of the ship, including the sick bay, wash-places and living spaces. August went slowly by, with gun trials, depth-charge-thrower trials, and a host of final inspections. Through it all the small naval party worked hard and began to learn their jobs.

They were the pathfinders. But, as the R.A.F. says affectionately of its lesser but no less necessary lights, 'After the pathfinders comes the shower'. For while the advance party worked hard to help bring the ship to top-line readiness, down in H.M.S. *Pembroke*, otherwise Royal Naval Barracks, Chatham, something was stirring. That something was a draft chit to a certain destroyer.

Chatham Barracks. Say that to an old Chatham rating. Fling in the stone and watch the ripples widen, ripples of a hundred assorted memories: of coaling-party, kit-musters and 'men under punishment to muster', of draft leave and crafty trips up the line to the Smoke, of short week-ends and 'Friday whiles', of smuggling 'rabbits' out to flog ashore, of P.O.'s messman and depot-school sweeper, of loafing in the heads or with an outgoing draft in the drill shed, or dodging the 'Gestapo'. Chatham Barracks, that great Victorian pile, that gentle penitentiary where many a mother's boy has broken his heart, where only the heart that turns to stone, or fiddles a cushy number in the Drafting Office, could survive. Ah, Chatham, and flat beer in the leading-hands' canteen; bangers and chips and fresh buttered bread on pay-day! This is the ancient home of the barrack stanchion, of Charles Causley's chief petty officer, that ancient mariner, 'more permanent than the spider in the enormous wall', whose

> . . . barefoot, coal-burning soul
> Expands, puffs like a toad, in the convict air
> Of the Royal Naval Barracks.

Of course, to the realist this is all-my-eye. All you have to do is to be nice to the chiefs and petty officers or find a convenient, long-lost oppo in the Central Regulating Office, a bloke you haven't seen since the old 'Q.E.', and sooner or later you'll get your soft number. Then you will make a million cups of tea for the Chief and grow fat on canteen grub. You'll even get well known at Aggie Weston's and the Salvation Army.

In that summer of 1939 the draft chits began to fly for the new ship. Long lists of names began to appear on the notice-boards in the drill shed opposite the Drafting Office, and anxious faces, that rapidly became either as long as fiddles or as happy as chief stokers off watch, scanned the tall columns for their names and numbers. Able seamen with hard-won sinecures would come into the mess for their tots, read the little *billets doux* and go pale, or swear, or merely shrug their shoulders philosophically. Barrack stanchions, whom hastily promised tots of neaters could not save, crumbled in a matter of minutes. Old stripeys were winkled out of obscure offices, and somebody else had to make the tea. Young ordinary seamen thrilled with pride and drove their seniors mad with their excited demands for the inside dope on *Kelly* and her captain. An ageing petty officer, 'his narrow forehead ruffled by the Jutland wind', would find himself for the Nth and countless time assembling his meticulously preserved gear and stowing it all neatly away into an old kit-bag, stiff with deep-sea salt, bleached by the sun of many foreign drafts.

One young able seaman sneaked into the heads for a quiet 'burn'. He was drawing on the butt end he had saved from stand-easy, when an oppo came in with the same idea in mind.

' 'Ullo, wings,' said A.B. number one; 'what's the buzz then?'

'I've got a draft chit.'

'You 'aven't!'

'Not flippin' many I 'aven't.'

'What ship?'

'*Kelly.*'

'*Kelly?* Never 'erd of 'er.'

'Destroyer.'

'Destroyers? I've spit 'em.'

'Well, spit us a couple more, then – we're going to need 'em.'

In the Navy there is a formula for everything. Naval language especially, is a fine, formal dance with its set figures and conventions.

Petty Officer Bert Male came up from Chatham to join the sick-bay staff of *Kelly*. After the long and tiring train journey he arrived at Hebburn feeling much the worse for wear, with that stale, railway taste in the mouth and the insidious railway dirt making him long for a good bath and a change of clothes. As soon as he arrived on board he had his first insight into the sort of ship the *Kelly* was going to be. He was met by the Medical Officer, who told him to have a wash and brush-up straight away and get a good meal inside him.

It was a standing rule of Captain Mountbatten's that he

saw every man who joined the ship as soon as he came aboard. So, after his meal, and feeling three times the man who had crawled out of the train, Bert met his Commanding Officer for the first time. Lord Louis Mountbatten welcomed him to the ship, and it was soon obvious that he knew Male's service background almost as well as Bert did himself. And what was more, he seemed interested.

Bert's experience was not unique, for every man who came aboard was interviewed in the same way. One able seaman thought that shaking hands with Lord Louis Mountbatten was something to write home about, and he did. They all wrote home about it. They all wrote that this ship seemed to be a home-from-home, with a Commanding Officer who could find time and enthusiasm both to acquaint himself with each man's background and personality and at the same time to put them in the picture as to what was expected of them aboard his ship. This personal interest in the men and their welfare was quickly noted. No man had been aboard the *Kelly* for long before he felt that in Captain Mountbatten he had a skipper he could trust, admire and follow blindly, no matter where he led; and in the *Kelly* a ship that he could look on as his second home as well as his place of work. That is the sort of ship a good sailor prays for. That is the sort of ship the *Kelly* was, from her very beginning throughout her entire career.

And even now they noticed something else about her. Personality will make itself felt, and remembered, in a very short space of time. A beautiful woman will work her fascination from the very moment she enters a room. She becomes the centre of attraction wherever she goes and whatever she does. She is unique and unforgettable and no one comes in contact with her who is not richer for the experience. The *Kelly* was like that.

Bert Male's job was, of course, in the ship's sick bay. After a brief look round the ship he began organising his department. Under the Surgeon Lieutenant he was responsible for the treatment and medical care of the *Kelly*'s ship's company, plus the overall superintendence of medical arrangements in the other ships of the flotilla as they were completed and came into service. In addition, he was in charge of the medical records and the medical stores. There was plenty of work to do, and the next few weeks would bring a great deal more.

Meanwhile, other members of the new ship's company were joining. You would see two or three new faces every day, and sometimes an old one. That would be an occasion for sippers, even gulpers, when tot time came round.

Gordon Rogers had been drafted to Chatham. There he and twenty-six other 'green hands' were put into the charge of a petty officer. He took one look at the class, heaved a huge sigh of despair, and said:

'Thank God Hitler can't see *you* or he'd attack right away.'

They felt flattered. It was the petty officer's unenviable job to make sailors out of these young and tender civilians, and he felt entitled to let off steam.

'Can any son of a sea-cook among you swim?' he bellowed.

Rogers plucked up courage and answered:

'Yes, sir, I can, sir, only I'm not the son of a sea-cook.'

His mentor came slowly and menacingly across and stood in front of him, those gentle eyes not three inches from Rogers' face.

'And what's your name?' he asked softly.

'Rogers, sir. . . .'

'Don't call me "sir". "P.O." is the way you will address me in future. Got *that*?' The roar filled the parade-ground and echoed back off the wall of the drill shed. The eyes were no longer gentle. They were fires of hate.

'So you can swim, eh, sonny?' The soft, silken voice again.

'Yes, P.O.' He was taking no chances this time.

'And you're not the son of a sea-cook?'

'No, sir . . . P.O.'

'Then perhaps you're the son of a *carrier*. Well, grab that sandbag and *carry* it above your head round the parade-ground at the double until I tell you to stop!' Rogers hesitated. 'At the DOUBLE!' The voice this time was like all the sirens on all the ships that ever rolled into one shattering blast. Rogers doubled off with the sandbag. When at last he felt he could hold it no longer he was called back. 'Well, Rogers, and what are you?'

'The son of a sea-cook . . . P.O.'

'Good, that's settled then. We'll see if you can swim tomorrow.' Then he turned to the class. 'Those of you who fancy they can swim, paddle, float or otherwise disport your filthy bodies in the 'ogwash will give me your names and you will be taking your swimming test tomorrow.'

They dismissed for dinner (bangers, pusser's duff and café-au-bromide). After dinner they fell in again, and until four o'clock explored the geography of the parade-ground, every blistering inch of it, marching and halting, marching and halting, until they learnt to halt on the command and not three paces later.

After a month of drill, of right turns, left turns, changing direction, left inclines, right inclines, forming squad, right wheels, left wheels, and anything else that professional hard heart could think up, they thought they knew the entire drill book, with variations. It was then that they were issued with rifles.

'Now,' said that man, 'we are going to learn rifle drill.'

The agony began again, only this time there was an extra weight to carry and drop and pick up. After the first few lessons Rogers was called to the front.

'Stoker Rogers will now demonstrate the correct way to slope arms.'

Rogers sloped and ordered arms on the command a

dozen times. The menace approached with the soft tread of an assassin.

'And where did you learn to do rifle drill before you joined the Andrew?'

'Me? Nowhere, P.O.'

'I see. Just come natural, eh?'

'Yes, P.O.'

'You're a fibber, sonny – a naughty, naughty fibber,' said the voice gently. 'So grab that rifle' – the wind rose to hurricane force – 'and do that again till I tell you to stop!'

From that day onwards, right through their rifle training, Rogers was the guinea-pig. Time and again he was dragged to the front and made to demonstrate whatever stage of drill they happened to have reached. Time and again came the same question, 'Where did you learn to do rifle drill?' with all the monotonous persistence of 'When did you last see your father?' But the inquisition could not last for ever. Finally they had their examination before the Disciplinary Officer and, to their amazement, received a recommend as the best class on parade. The man who had bullied, beaten and tormented them throughout that eternity of damnation stood them at ease for the last time and addressed them.

'Lads, you've done well. When you came to me you was civilians and you was a proper shower. I never saw such a bunch of bastards in my life as when you first picked up a rifle. But you learnt, and you've done well. Just remember this: whatever anybody else can do, the Navy can do it better. Next time you watch a big parade, watch the Guards go by and then look at the Navy. And if the lads aren't marching straighter and their dressing isn't better and everything else isn't better, I . . . ' He paused. ' . . . I am the Archangel Gabriel and you are my flaming 'arping party.' And they all knew better than that. But he hadn't finished.

'There's just one more thing. Rogers.'

'Yes, P.O.'

'Please, Rogers, where did you learn rifle drill before you joined the Navy?'

'I was five and a half years in the Territorial Army, P.O.'

'Thank you, Rogers. All right. Dismiss! Rogers.'

'Yes, P.O.'

'Come round to the mess after tot time tomorrow and I'll give you sippers.'

Before they moved on, the twenty-seven members of the class clubbed together and gave their late torturer a cigarette case, which they presented to him on their last day together.

'Thank you, lads. Just the job for my ticklers,' he said.

The next day they were placed in the charge of a stoker petty officer and taken to the Mechanical Training Establishment in Chatham dockyard, where they went through the second-class stoker's course. The next three months were all classroom work. Finally they passed out and were ready for sea.

Gordon was sitting in the mess one afternoon when a man came in asking for him.

'Your brother wants you to go aboard to see him – he's duty watch and can't come ashore,' he said.

Rogers went ashore that evening in his best suit. He met his brother at the top of the gangway of his ship.

'Where the hell did you get that suit?' was the reception. 'It's blooming terrible.'

Next day the sprog stoker was taken ashore to a naval outfitter's and introduced to the splendours and miseries of a tiddley suit.

Not that he was completely ignorant of how a well-dressed matelot should look. He had seen his brothers in uniform often enough, and he knew something about the 'Bell-bottom trousers, coat of navy blue', soon to be 'Climbing up the rigging like his father used to do'. But he could hardly be blamed for being a mere apprentice to the trade and art of naval *haute couture*, for real knowledge comes only with experience.

A matelot's collar, to begin with, is like an iceberg, with nine-tenths of its bulk below the surface. The gay blue square, with its three white stripes round the edge, that you see flaring up crisply out of the tight jumper, is merely the fine flower. The part that the girl-friend sees and touches for luck (she'll need it) has deep roots – a long strip reaching down the back and two further strips down the chest to the waist, the whole being further complicated by two long white tapes to lash the apparatus round the middle. And you can never decide whether to tie the flaming thing inside or outside the trousers.

But gradually you learn. The stringy bow you wore on the side of your cap slides round to the front, right above the bridge of the nose, and grows in size and elegance – your 'eye-shooting' bow. The tapes on your jumper grow almost to your knees, and your silk is no longer sewn together at the ends, nor is it of the regulation width; its 'duffle-bag' disappears and the whole thing becomes flat and shiny, like a ribbon of blue-black steel that has just snaked out of the hydraulic press. You buy yourself a pair of black, shiny slippers with silver buckles from 'slops', and with these on your feet and long dark sideboards on your cheeks you begin to evoke memories of tarry pigtails, black boaters and striped jerseys. Of course the silver zips in the sides of your jumper were not worn at Trafalgar. During the war you were called a 'spiv' if you wore these, long before the word came into common civilian use. But these zips are not entirely ornamental. They help a matelot to divest himself of the tight jumper, and even then he has to have two oppos to help him, who peel it off his body like a skin off a rabbit, leaving him feeling that he has been severely keel-hauled.

The tiddley suit itself is an indispensable item in a well-dressed matelot's wardrobe, and an ordinary seaman acquires one as soon as possible. It is a skin-tight, flamboyant creation, with enormous bell-bottoms to the trousers and a jumper with a plunging neckline. The cuffs are buttoned, and ashore you usually wear them turned back. This, besides leaving your hands free to cope with any of the situations likely to arise on a run ashore, displays in its full glory the chromium-plated wrist-watch and strap that you wear as low down on your wrist as you can push them. In this natty suiting you learn to roll, to walk with shoulders hunched, and you acquire the matelot's permanent look of sour disgust. (The 'jolly tar' is a landsman's fiction. A matelot is always 'chokka block', 'proper chokka', or 'two-blocks, meself'.)

And by the time the tailor had finished with him Gordon Rogers was two-blocks, himself, though he had to admit to the glass that he looked a lot smarter. He even looked a bit like a matelot now, with his gold badge and reduced silhouette.

All this time he was watching the drafting notice-board, his mind full of the names of famous ships like the *Rodney*, *Nelson* and *Renown*. He wondered which one he would be drafted to. At last he saw his name on the list: G. A. Rogers, stoker second class. Alongside it was H.M.S. *Kelly*. He turned the name over in his mind, wondering what sort of a ship it could be. He felt disappointed.

'Seen off again,' he said and shrugged his shoulders.

That night he asked his brother about the *Kelly*.

'You lucky bastard,' was the reaction. 'She's a brand-new job and you've got the best skipper in the Navy.'

She looked a brand-new job, too, when he saw her a fortnight later, after ten days' draft leave and a long trip by special train to Hawthorn Leslie's yard at Hebburn-on-Tyne.

It was all very strange and intensely exciting. They arrived at Hebburn station about half-past four in the afternoon. There to meet the train was *Kelly*'s First Lieutenant, Lieutenant-Commander Burnett, who stood up on a luggage truck and told them something about their new ship. Their new 'home' he called it, with a grin. In fact he grinned all the time as he spoke, as if the whole affair were one huge joke. Then they fell in on the road outside the station and marched down to the dockyard.

Rogers had a funny feeling in his stomach as they marched through the gates and on through a forest of tall scaffolding, broken here and there by clearings where the keel-plates of new ships lay open to the sky. Suddenly, as they rounded a corner, he saw the river. Someone shouted:

'There she is!'

Rogers looked and saw his ship. It was his first ship, that pale-grey destroyer with the leader's proud band round her funnel, his home for the next two and a half years. He felt very proud at that moment. But he felt prouder still when he went aboard her, watched by the dockyard mateys.

When he got inboard he was a little disappointed at the state of untidiness which prevailed everywhere. The deck was littered like a junkyard with drums of oil and paint, wooden boxes and packing-cases, and air hoses for the pneumatic drills. He felt he wanted to roll up his sleeves there and then and clean up the rubbish. When they reached their messes they found an even greater state of chassis. Filling every inch of space were large packing-cases filled with straw and assorted mess-traps – the cups, saucers, plates, knives, forks and spoons, pots and pans necessary for cooking. But they all turned to and had it cleared away in no time. Then they had their tea and unpacked their personal gear, transferring it from kit-bags to shiny, clean new lockers. This done, the next job was to choose a good billet for slinging a hammock, preferably somewhere away from the gangway, a corner where the bosun's mate could not pump you out of sleep as he passed underneath on his way to shake reliefs. It was while they were busy with this that the Chief Stoker came down and told them their duties. He gave them their station cards, which told them their part of watch for duty and leave, their defence, cruising, and action stations.

It was bewildering, but there was worse to come. Chiefie advised all the new men to go round the ship and, in particular, to make themselves familiar with the boiler- and engine-rooms.

Down below, Gordon wandered through the fantastic nightmare garden of the machinery. He felt very small, a helpless midget lost in the immensity and complexity of it all. Why didn't I go for signals after all, he asked himself miserably.

But the new second-class stoker was by no means the only man aboard who gave uneasy thought to the future. There were worries enough aft, as well as for'ard.

The *Kelly*'s Wardroom faced a heavy responsibility. Other officers could be merely efficient. They must be perfection. That black band round the funnel had a special meaning for them. They had to lead the flotilla; they had to set an example.

And as if that wasn't enough to have on one's plate, there was Mountbatten. They all knew what his standards were and what he demanded from his men.

'He doesn't ask for miracles,' said one lieutenant, 'but he's bloody disappointed if they don't happen.'

'I can feel my ulcer licking its lips,' said another, staring into the depths of his large pink gin with the look of a would-be suicide into the Thames.

Of course their records showed that they were all first-class men. They wouldn't have got here at all if they had not been the best. All the same, it was going to be tricky.

Especially for Lieutenant Dunsterville. 'Dusty' Dunsterville was the *Kelly*'s Signals Officer, and, better than most, he knew Mountbatten's reputation in the Signals Branch. He would be working under the eyes of the man who, more than any other officer, had helped to raise naval communications to the state of high efficiency it could now boast. Dunsterville, if he had them, could be excused a few qualms at the thought of the opposition. But he had a few weapons at his command. In fact, he had the two essentials of naval life. He knew his job and he could take a joke. His messmates soon found out that he could give one, too.

The wardroom bristled with specialists. Lieutenant-Commander Burnett, the First Lieutenant, was a brilliant officer. Besides being responsible for running the ship's internal economy and general organisation, he also ruled the Asdic cabinet. Burnett's ambition for his own trade demanded a sacrifice of U-boats, and he only hoped that, if war came, the Nazis would help him to a testimonial by presenting him with plenty of 'pings'. What Burnett hoped to do to undersea marauders, Lieutenant Robin and Goodenough had every confidence of doing those that came on the surface. Robin was a gunnery expert with a whole range of new weapons in his charge. A baby would have preferred candy, and Lieutenant Goodenough preferred his torpedo-tubes. The *Kelly* was better than a Tribal in that respect. He would have ten of them to play with, ten 'sardines' per broadside – as many as the fingers of his hands and adding up to quite a punch. He hoped there would be something big to hit – a pocket battleship perhaps.

They were all experts, these men, but neither Burnett with his groping Asdics, nor Robin with his pom-poms and 4·7s, nor yet Goodenough with his deadly, dark-blue fish, could ever hope to smite the enemy without the man whose calculations would bring them to the right place to do it. A flotilla navigator has to be a very good navigator. Maurice Butler-Bowdon was outstanding. Not only first-rate in skill, he was the very soul of application and energy.

The *Kelly* was a challenge to them all. She could break them. But she could also make them. Every man realised that here was his big chance, that he would probably never get a better. They could not afford to throw it away; they could not afford to make mistakes.

The hour of departure was nearly at hand, but before the ship finally cast off the ship's company were given shore leave. In that one run ashore many of them made the acquaintance of Tyneside haunts they were to get to know so much better at a later date – pubs like The Commercial, half-way up Ellison Street from Hawthorn's, and home-from-homes like the R.A.O.B. Club in Jarrow.

It was at the R.A.O.B. Club that Gordon Rogers introduced Tyneside to his musical talents. Gordon's hobby was singing to a ukelele. He had a large repertoire of songs, a collection which grew daily as he listened to some of the saltier party pieces of his more experienced messmates. He and the warm-hearted Geordies found that they had two important loves in common – a good sing-song and a glass of beer. There was plenty of both at the R.A.O.B.

There were places, too, like the Power House dance hall, where Jack showed the lively Tynesiders that a quickstep is the modern matelot's hornpipe. Of course beer and skittles cost money, and entertaining the Geordie lasses cost more. Some of the men had got a foot in the door before they left barracks and had managed to get a 'casual'. But many were flat broke, and a casual doesn't go very far, anyway. The poor men borrowed from the rich men, and some got an advance. One man plucked up courage and approached the First Lieutenant for a 'rubber'.

'Certainly. How much?' said Jimmy-the-One.

'Could I have ten pounds?' asked the man. 'I'm a bit short.'

'Well, don't come to me if you're a *lot* short, that's all,' said Jimmy.

The rating wrote out his I.O.U. for ten pounds and handed it over. Burnett looked at it, grinned and added a second nought to the figure.

'You'll be had one of these fine days if you make out an I.O.U. like that,' he said.

They had their run ashore and came back happy in the

knowledge that Hebburn belonged to them. Even when they fell in next morning and were detailed off to their various jobs, they came to the conclusion amongst themselves that the Geordies were 'all right'. Some of them had received invitations to come and make themselves at home, and a few were 'up homers' already. The beer was good, too.

When the hands were called on the morning of August 23rd it was for something more than merely 'part of ship'. They and the dockyard mateys cast off, and the *Kelly* left the jetty. As she steamed slowly down the Tyne, a pale sunlight caught the gleam of her bright paintwork and picked out the flotilla leader's proud black band round the top of the funnel. It was the day of her acceptance trials and there was not a single man who did not feel proud to be aboard her. They needed no further evidence of her quality. They knew she was a good 'un, and so did her builders.

She passed slowly down river, past the clanging shipyards and the ships lining the stream. She passed Tyne Dock and Jarrow Staithes, the Pilot House and the dreaded Black Middens. Slowly she left the ugly black rocks to port. Then it was a matter of minutes before her bull-ring passed the piers and her bows tasted North Sea salt again. She seemed to sniff the air, taste the sharp salt and feel the tang of the breeze. Then she was off, her course set for the measured mile, a gentle smoke haze coming from her proud, raking funnel.

At the other end of the smoke Commander Evans and his men were on their mettle, and so were the new engines.

Rogers had the afternoon watch, from noon until four. In his eagerness he went down into the boiler-room at five-past eleven. But the stoker petty officer on watch soon chased him out.

'Go and have a walk, son – you're miles too early,' he laughed.

Gordon went on to the upper deck and walked nervously up and down. A leading stoker came up and started chatting. Gordon told him he had been run out of the boiler-room.

'You won't be so eager in six months' time,' laughed the leading hand. 'Come and get your dinner. You're on my watch this afternoon. You can come down with me at five to twelve – and not a minute before!'

The ship was well under way when he reached the boiler-room for his first watch in the Navy. He arrived on the floorplates to find three men from the dockyard in occupation. In fact the builders were still in command everywhere. The Navy had not yet taken delivery.

On the measured mile she showed her paces, and finally confirmed everything that Admiralty specifications had demanded, everything that the cunning skill of Tyneside hands and brains had put into that splendid, slender hull and the magnificent machinery that drove her now like a hungry shark through the choppy water, easily outpacing the official speed.

Finally, after six hours of gruelling tests, the moment came for the change of ownership. The Red Duster was hauled down and the White Ensign broken aboard for the first time.

At that moment the new order came into being below. Gordon had been watching the firm's representative doing the job he would soon have to do. Then the dockyard man turned his head.

'Right, she's all yours, lad,' he said.

It was like a pilot going solo for the first time. The dockyard man showed him how to manipulate the damper, how to light or extinguish a sprayer as more or less steam was required.

'All you have to do,' he said to a tense but determined Rogers, 'is to pull out your damper, turn on your oil and flash it by shoving the damper in and pulling it out quickly. There's an art in it, but you look as if you'll pick it up in no time.'

'How does it work, then?' asked Gordon, stalling for time.

'Well,' said the other man, with a fatherly twinkle in his eye, 'when you do all that with the damper you cut off the air supply and then bring it back quickly. That makes the flame from the other sprayers shoot across to the sprayer you've just turned on and light it. That gives you more steam to send across to the main engines and drive the ship faster through the water.'

'Thanks,' said Gordon. 'I'll have a go next time, then.'

And as the Navy took over from the dockyard, builder and Captain put pen to paper. One piece of paper affirmed that

> We, Messrs Hawthorn, Leslie & Co. Ltd, Hebburn-on-Tyne, at/off The Tyne handed over this twenty-third day of August, one thousand nine hundred and thirty-nine, at 3.30 p.m. o'clock, H.M.S. *Kelly*, constructed by us for His Majesty's Navy.

Its companion, which is still on the files of the firm, agreed that His Majesty's Navy, represented by the signature 'Louis Mountbatten, Captain, Royal Navy',

> Received from Messrs Hawthorn, Leslie & Co. Ltd, Hebburn-on-Tyne, H.M.S. *Kelly*, this twenty-third day of August, one thousand nine hundred and thirty-nine, without prejudice to outstanding liabilities.

They shook hands and the thing was done, signed and settled. The *Kelly* was part of the Royal Navy. All that was left of her business up on this great northern river was a quick but triumphant trip back to Hebburn to land the builders' representatives and pick up a few more of her ship's company who had arrived from Chatham. Then she turned out to sea again and this time her course was charted for the south.

CHAPTER III

THE BALLOON GOES UP

'EGG' BURNETT, First Lieutenant and ping expert, had one very pronounced peculiarity. The sheer inefficiency of most men is usually anything but funny to those who have to lead them, but to the Egg it was a riot. It was a pretty safe bet that if Egg laughed you had done *something* wrong.

One day, just before the ship's trials started, Burnett and Primrose, who was the duty petty officer, had gone below into the seamen's messdeck to try and find the best places to fix the ammunition chutes that linked magazines with guns. It was a tricky problem. The chutes would have to occupy space on the messdecks, and they had to be fitted where nothing could interfere with their smooth working in action. They had a good look round. At first sight there seemed to be plenty of places where the chutes could be stowed.

'Yes, they'd fit in all right when they weren't in use,'

worried Burnett, 'but all this mess gear would get in the way when they were rigged for action.'

'In that case, sir, there's nothing to worry about; they'll never *be* in action, except for exercises and that,' said Primrose.

The Egg looked up. His eyes twinkled. The twinkle became a grin and the grin set light to a roar of laughter.

'P.O.,' he said, with the air of 'this one'll kill you', 'P.O., when we put to sea they'll *always* be in action.'

So much mirth was infectious. The petty officer grinned.

'Why, when's the war going to break out then, sir?' he said.

'If my guess is any good,' said Burnett, 'the damn balloon is about to go up at any minute.'

And by that time only the woolliest optimist, wearing the rosiest of rose-coloured glasses, could possibly think otherwise.

Once again tension had mounted in Europe, and this time it was obvious that there would be no more Munichs. On August 24th Mr Chamberlain declared, at an emergency meeting of Parliament, 'We find ourselves confronted with the imminent peril of war.' The immediate event which had prompted this statement had occurred on the previous day. On the 23rd, the very day that the *Kelly* became a unit of the Royal Navy, a German Gauleiter was proclaimed head of the State in the 'free' city of Danzig.

Danzig was the Sarajevo of the new crisis. But this new act of German treachery was only the climax to the steady goose-step of German aggression that had marched rapidly on since the short honeymoon period after Munich. Czechoslovakia was the first victim. On March 15th the German army occupied Prague. Hitler tore up the Munich agreement and Czechoslovakia was no more. A week later he presented Lithuania with an ultimatum demanding the surrender of Memelland. His demand was immediately complied with.

These easy victories gave the lesser bandit the courage he needed, and on April 7th Italy invaded Albania. Very soon another head had fallen. Meanwhile Hitler had turned his hungry eyes on Poland. In Danzig the Fuehrer had found another Sudetenland. The free city was the sea outlet for Polish overseas trade. Its population was mainly German, and through this majority the Nazis gradually assumed control over the Danzig Senate. Closely tied to Danzig in German desires was the Polish province of Pomorze, the 'Corridor' that separated East Prussia from the Reich. By the end of March German pressure on Poland had become so intolerable, following on the Czechoslovakian grab and Hitler's persistent, hysterical abuse of Britain and France for their rearmament policies and 'antagonism' to his designs on Europe, that the two governments, on March 31st, made a pledge to Poland to support her in the event of an attack by Germany. A month later a bill for the introduction of conscription was passed in the House of Commons. The situation in Poland went from bad to worse. In mid-August the German puppet government in Danzig began to prevent Polish customs officials from carrying out their duties. Poland warned the Danzig Senate; Germany warned Poland. A German nominee assumed supreme power in the Senate, and the Nazis increased their campaign of hate against Poland. The Pope, President Roosevelt and the King of the Belgians all broadcast appeals for peace. But war seemed now inevitable. In Britain the temper of the people had slowly but surely developed into a hatred of the maniac Hitler and all he stood for. Everywhere the feeling smouldered, under the surface of doubt and indecision, that the last word had been said, the last piece of paper signed.

As the *Kelly* finished her trials and went into service the Navy was mobilised. The Reserve Fleet was called up for combined sea and air exercises, and the whole fighting strength of the Navy went to sea, ostensibly on 'exercises' in the North Sea, in reality disposed so as to face any eventuality. Ahead of the main fleet the destroyers watched the sea and searched the waters below for the enemy. It would not be long now before the *Kelly* joined them.

She left the Tyne and steamed south. In the ship's office Bob Knight still dreamed his bright Mediterranean dream, but by now he had little hope left of seeing it come true – not for a long time, at any rate. He knew only too well that a crack new fighting ship like the *Kelly* would be sent wherever the action was likely to be hottest. With Germany in the war it would be an easy guess as to where that would be. With U-boats watching the convoy routes and merchant-raiders poised to fall on our shipping, the *Kelly*'s new guns and torpedo tubes would be at a premium – in home waters. So goodbye Malta and awnings spread in the sun; goodbye Valetta and Jose's little bar where the ambit flowed; goodbye . . . for the duration. But the dream would be something to hold on to, like the thought of peace. His duties also helped to push the sunlit vision farther into the background. In addition to his normal duties, Knight had become a newspaperman. His 'column' was the *K Destroyer Flotilla*, or *K.D.F.*, *News*, a broadcast which was to cover local events in the new flotilla. It was firmly stressed by the 'proprietors' of the *K.D.F. News* that the paper was to be a *daily* – and with a war coming on, too! The editor went to work with a firm determination that the 'daily' should never miss a day. It never did.

So towards the end of that uneasy summer the destroyer reached her depot, Chatham. She berthed in the dockyard, and immediately the remainder of the ship's company joined her from barracks. They assembled in the drill shed and were marched out to the ship. To most of them she looked a smart, tiddley ship as they caught their first sight of her.

'Nobby' Clarke examined her critically. She looked a

little bit like a light cruiser with her twin mountings and elaborate bridge. But the flare of her bows, the rake of masts and funnels, indicated her function only too clearly to an old hand. She looked what she was – the finest ship of her class afloat. Her appearance was slightly spoiled, however, by a fleet of barges that had assembled round her in the stream. But that didn't worry Petty Officer Clarke very much. He was pleased with his new draft, which had come as a result of volunteering for a foreign draft some weeks before. Nobby had served aboard the training battleship *Royal Sovereign* as a boys' instructor just long enough to 'brown him off up to the eyebrows'. In naval language he was 'two blocks' with teaching boys, and a brand-new destroyer bound for the 'Med' on a two-and-a-half-year commission looked just the sort of change he needed. 'Just suit me a treat,' he said to himself.

The new men were met by the Chief Boatswain's Mate and the Chief Gunner's Mate (to them 'the Buffer' and the 'G.I.'), who gave out station cards and directed them to their messes.

As soon as the men were aboard, 'Clear Lower Deck' was piped. Various buzzes were circulating by this time. Some swore that the *Kelly* was still bound for the 'Med', after her normal working-up trials. Others had the story that the ship was to take the King and Queen to Belgium. So it was with unusual curiosity that the hands mustered. Captain Mountbatten began.

'In my experience,' he said, 'I have always found that you cannot have an efficient ship unless you have a happy ship, and you cannot have a happy ship unless you have an efficient ship. That is the way I intend to start this commission, and that is the way I intend to go on – with a happy and an efficient ship.'

The younger members present felt a surge of confidence at his words and an instinctive determination to live up to them. Some of the older hands preferred to 'wait and see about that', but there was no one present who did not feel that the commission was getting off to a good start. Then came the information they were all waiting for.

'We have come to Chatham,' Mountbatten went on, 'to store and ammunition ship. Now, normally we are allowed three weeks by the Admiralty to complete this operation. I have decided that it must be completed in three days. I expect you all to play your part irrespective of whether you are a stoker or a seaman, a writer or a cook. We have a job to do. Let's do it.'

There was a general murmur and an exchange of startled looks as the Captain finished his remarks. The motto of the *Kelly* was 'Keep On', he told them, and he expected them to live up to it.

Some of the sprogs were visibly shaken. One young seaman turned round in disgust.

'If this is the *Kelly* I'm getting a draft chit before this three-days lark can get started,' he said. 'Keep on, eh! His Lordship ain't kidding, is he?'

The hands then discovered what all the attendant barges were for. They contained stores, and, most disheartening of all, ammunition. But they all turned to and worked hard, humping sides of beef, shells and various brands of 'pusser's stores' up over the side, along the decks and down into the empty spaces below. They 'kept on' for three days and nights of backbreaking work, snatching sleep when they could and only breaking off for a bite to eat and a cup of 'ky'. And they finished the job, though a matelot would not be a matelot without dripping a bit at the area. What a way to spend your first day aboard ship!

One thing was certain now. War was coming, and any day might see them at action stations. With this atmosphere intensifying daily, the *Kelly* left Chatham on August 29th and sailed for Portland for her working-up trials.

Rogers had had the last dog watch on the floorplates, and he took a turn on deck before slinging his hammock.

It was a beautiful, moonlit night. Away to starboard,

across the dark water, the lights of the seaside towns cast their bright gleam upon a calm sea. Everywhere there was the hush of peace. The slow rhythm of the ship's motion seemed as fixed and inevitable as the path of the moon round the earth. To Rogers it seemed as if he had always been here, in this swaying ship, poised between glittering sea and darkening sky, her bows aimed at that unknown horizon made shadowy and intangible by the mystery of dusk.

He went for'ard and perched himself on 'A' gun, on the convenient seat formed by the break in the gun-shield between the long barrels of the guns. He watched the bows dip and rise; he felt the mass of the heavy ship under him and the tremor of the engines running through it like a pulse; he heard the gentle swish of the bow wave. The twin projectories of the guns seemed to converge on some predestined target ahead, although, like railway lines, their urgent journeys would never meet. He looked into the evening and felt quite alone on the sea. But it was getting cold. He jumped down and walked aft. Round the funnel on the iron deck a group was gathered drinking cocoa. He joined them and listened to the old-timers spinning yarns, weaving a picture of the old, peacetime Navy. The cocoa warmed his body, and as he sipped it and listened to tales of the China Station and the warm Mediterranean he felt that he had struck his place in life, that this was just the life for him.

On the way down everyone made efforts to acclimatise themselves to the new ship and to their new routine. Nobby Clarke began to settle down to his new job. Any petty officer who has ever done the job will agree that the 'petty officer in charge messdecks and flats' has plenty to drip about. It is known in the Navy as one of the world's worst jobs and that was the number that Nobby collected. He was soon at loggerheads with the First Lieutenant.

'It's like trying to get blood out of a stone, getting hands out of Jimmy for cleaning up the flats. As often as not I'm on my hands and knees scrubbing out when my sweeper's on watch at defence stations,' he moaned to his oppos in the P.O.s' mess. He was merely repeating, with one or two variations, a speech that has been made at one time or another aboard almost every ship in the Navy ever since there were messdecks and flats to scrub out and petty officers to watch over them.

At Portland the working-up trials began immediately, and life aboard became one continuous, hectic round of speed trials, practice shoots with the new armament and all the headaches, heartaches and backaches that are inseparable from the gruelling job of bringing a new ship and a new crew to the degree of fighting efficiency that her captain demanded. To make things worse, all this, like the marathon at Chatham, had to be done in a fraction of the time normally allowed. If there wasn't a war on, it was only just round the corner.

The first practice shoot of the main armament shattered the apple-pie order of the new gear in the messdecks. Cups, plate and mess-traps were flung across the deck, and things were no longer Bristol fashion below. When the watch came back into the for'ard messdeck they thought they saw a big white rat chasing its own tail round and round under the table. It was the ship's cat, christened 'Hawthorn' in affectionate memory of her builders, and now 'christened' again by a bag of flour that had fallen from the shelf and burst all over her.

The pom-pom went into action against sleeve targets, and the ship's anti-aircraft section very nearly notched up its first kill. On this particular day the Royal Air Force pilot in the towing aircraft had already taken his life in his hands during four runs past the ship, when on the next running of the gauntlet a lucky shot parted the tow wire and the target fluttered down into the sea. A party of stokers off watch who were grouped near the funnel watching the fun let out a hearty cheer and someone shouted, 'Why should England tremble when old Stripey is is behind the gun.' What the Royal Air Force said on that occasion is not recorded.

Nobody yet quite realised the grim purpose of these speeded-up trials, which was perhaps just as well. The main justification for the exercises was being proved – they were learning their jobs. In the boiler-room Rogers was finding plenty to interest him and keep him happy. In a letter home he wrote: 'I can put those sprayers on or knock them off while you wink.' On his action station, too, he was satisfied that he knew his job. As an ammunition supply number he had to take the shells off the hoist as they came up from the magazine and carry them over to the next hoist, where they were shot up to the gun's crew. As well as mastering his job, Rogers, like many others on board, was getting his sea legs. For the *Kelly* was getting in as much sea-time as she could in preparation for the real test.

They were at sea when the signal came. Petty Officer Primrose read it when it came into the wireless office and took the message straight to the Captain. The signal read:

> General from Admiralty. Fuse all shell, ship all warheads.

The state of emergency had entered its final stage. Summer was over and peace hung rotten on the branch.

After divisions that Sunday the Captain called all the officers, chief and petty officers together to give them a lecture on the station-keeping device of his own invention which was fitted aboard the ship. He described briefly the principles behind the working of his gear, and he was coming to the end of his remarks, when the door opened and Petty Officer Primrose came in. He walked up to the Captain and handed him a slip of paper.

'Excuse me, sir. This signal has just come in.'

There was a pause, and a breathless silence while Lord Mountbatten read the signal. Then, with a brief

'Thank you,' he put the slip of paper into his pocket and looked at his audience.

'This is the stage in my lecture,' he said, 'at which I usually point out how valuable the automatic station-keeper would be in wartime, when the captain and the other officers on the bridge have so many things to do besides keeping the ship in station on the other ships of the flotilla. I usually say, "Now I have given you the basic principles of operating my gear. If war should at this moment break out, you know enough about it to work it." ' He paused. 'Well, war has at this moment broken out'

The signal read:

> From Admiralty to all concerned at home and abroad. Most Immediate. Commence hostilities at once with Germany.

The lecture party immediately broke up and before long the news was all over the ship. Then the 'still' was piped and the Captain's voice was heard over the ship's broadcasting system.

'There is no need for me to tell you what you already know,' he said, 'but one thing I will tell you. When we leave the shelter of this harbour we shall be right in the face of the enemy, who will be out to destroy us. We must therefore find him and destroy him first.'

After the broken voice of Mr Chamberlain had been heard on the radio, all hands were mustered to perform a melancholy task. They were told off to paint ship. They soon had stages, boats and catamarans out all round the ship's side and, foot by foot, the beautiful pale grey enamel that the builders had taken such pains over was covered with the ugly dark grey of Home Fleet colours. Everyone on board took a brush and helped with the desecration, officers as well as ratings, 'all hands and the cook'. On Petty Officer Clarke's catamaran were two seamen and Lord Mountbatten himself, resplendent in white overalls and painting away as hard as anyone, slapping the dull 'crab fat' on that gleaming hull. The work went on rapidly, with the Captain and his officers setting the example, though those beautiful white overalls were not so white after the other members of the Mountbatten catamaran's crew had given them one or two crafty sloshes when their owner wasn't looking.

The job was finished by dinner-time and leave was piped for all hands who could be spared. Most of them made for the White Ensign Club in Portland and did their best to wash down the paint fumes. Hitler was toasted in beer, and many unkind remarks were made about the paper-hanger's character and the morals of his nearest and dearest. Non-stop buzzes circulated, all purporting to be the latest, foolproof, exclusive, inside information on the *Kelly*'s immediate future. A few alcoholic tears were shed for the memory of that lovely Mediterranean cruise that never came off, the far-off happy time that had been finally obliterated that forenoon. The glittering map of a matelot's dream lay covered with thick grey pusser's paint.

But the *Kelly* was still the *Kelly,* and beauty is only skin-deep. She was still a good ship, they said over their beer, was their 'little grey home in the west'. When they came off leave that night they knew that they had probably had their last good run ashore under the lights of peace.

'Well,' said one old A.B., 'it was good while it lasted.'

'Ah,' said his oppo from the depths of an empty beer mug, 'the condemned man ate a hearty breakfast.'

The following day the war really began for the *Kelly.* They left harbour early for training in company with another destroyer, the *Acheron*, and a motor anti-submarine boat. Before they left, however, the Captain spoke to them again.

'We are going out for anti-submarine exercises this morning,' he informed them, and went on to warn, 'I shall have lookouts posted and shall deal severely with any man who does not keep a proper lookout.'

Not long after leaving harbour the anti-submarine boat, which was about a mile and a half away from the *Kelly,* suddenly signalled: 'Torpedoes approaching you.' *Kelly* was immediately manoeuvred to place her stern towards the M.A.S.B. so as to reduce her target, since the torpedoes must have passed close to the M.A.S.B. for her to have seen them. A broadcast was immediately made aboard the *Kelly* instructing anyone who sighted torpedoes to shout instantly to the bridge. Meanwhile the *Kelly's* Asdics immediately went into action and the three ships started a search of the area. At that point a man came up to the bridge and said:

'You didn't mean the torpedoes fired by the M.A.S.B. when you made that broadcast a few minutes ago, did you, sir?'

He was immediately and forcibly reminded that it was not his job to consider where torpedoes came from but to report any tracks sighted at once, and, further, that as an M.A.S.B. did not carry torpedoes those he had sighted must have been from a submarine.

Then the *Kelly* got a 'ping'. She steamed straight over the position indicated and dropped a pattern of depth charges, her first offensive action of the war. The *Acheron* followed close astern and dropped another pattern. The ships steamed over the area again and all hands searched the surface of the sea for signs of wreckage. They were rewarded by the sight of several large patches of oil fuel. The ship stopped to take a sample of it.

But oil was by no means the only thing that the exploding depth charges brought to the surface. The sea was littered with dead, half-dead and stunned fish of every variety. One man, who happened to be the ship's postman, saw a large cod floating alongside. With great presence of mind he grabbed a boat-hook and hauled the big fish inboard. When it was weighed the fish was found to register over forty pounds. The for'ard messdeck had a tasty meal of fish next day.

The stokers' mess, too, did well out of *Kelly*'s and the *Acheron*'s 'probable'. Two stokers from opposite messes sighted another huge fish and both tried to catch it in buckets made fast to the ends of heaving lines. One man managed to get his bucket round the fish and with a victorious shout of 'It's mine! I've got it!' began to haul it slowly up the ship's side. But disaster overtook him in the shape of a scupper which caught the edge of the bucket and upturned the fish into the sea. The other stoker, an Irishman, promptly lowered his bucket over the side and caught it again. He was more successful than his mate, and when he hauled the fish inboard all the stokers off watch followed him in a victory procession down to the messdeck. There a fierce argument began between the two fishermen as to which one was the rightful owner. Paddy got fed up with the argument and glared at the other man.

'Do you want the ruddy fish?' he shouted.

'Yes. It's mine, anyway.'

'Well, take it,' yelled Paddy. He swung his arm and landed the trophy with a loud, wet smack right between the other man's eyes. The unlucky fisherman toppled over backwards and lay on the messdeck with the codfish draped artistically across his chest, looking himself a little bit like the one that got away. Pandemonium broke out on the messdeck, which threatened to become a free fight between the two messes, until the leading hand of Paddy's mess intervened and made them share it. Even then there was plenty for everybody. And the other messes had not been idle. That night everyone turned to for a little spud-bashing, and a slap-up supper of fish and chips – on Hitler – was enjoyed by all hands.

This day's work was, of course, wonderful copy for Bob Knight and his *K.D.F. News.* No. 11 of that top-selling daily, for Tuesday, September 5th, 1939, commented on the incident from several aspects and read as follows:

YESTERDAY'S PROGRAMME

That's War – that was; but we must not lead ourselves to believe that some of the catch will always appear on the breakfast-table. The presence of mind of Posty in producing a gaff to lift the whales inboard while the ship had stopped to obtain a sample of the oil on the sea is much to be admired. We all hope that the *Kelly*'s and *Acheron*'s efforts did away with one of the pests that sank, without warning, the liner *Athenia* on Sunday night – and, of course, we hope that the lucky messes in the *Kelly* enjoyed their breakfast.

There is plenty of corroborative evidence to show that there were two U-boats here yesterday – one in Weymouth Bay and one in West Bay. The periscope of the former was seen from the signal bridge of the *Resolution* and the M.A.S.B. saw the tracks of two torpedoes fired at the *Kelly*. They only missed us by thirty or forty yards, so that we certainly were lucky. Only eight men of the *Kelly* saw the tracks, but as they seemed to think that the M.A.S.B. had fired the torpedoes at us for practice they were not as worried as they ought to have been. IT MUST BE STRESSED AGAIN THAT WHENEVER ANYBODY SEES A PERISCOPE OR TORPEDO TRACK THEY MUST DRAW THE BRIDGE'S ATTENTION TO THIS AT ONCE, EVEN IF IT MEANS YELLING AND SCREAMING THE PLACE DOWN.

To be missed by one submarine and bag another all in the first day's was is good going.

TODAY'S PROGRAMME

We are remaining in harbour today, at all events until the evening, because efficient working up demands occasional days in harbour to prepare the ground work.

The mention of the *Athenia* struck a tragic note. The sinking of this liner on the first day of hostilities shocked the British people deeply and showed them right away what sort of an enemy they were fighting.

On the evening of September 3rd the *Athenia,* a Donaldson liner of 13,581 tons, was outward bound for Montreal with fourteen hundred people aboard. She was in a position two hundred and fifty miles west of Ireland when she was torpedoed without warning and sunk with heavy loss of life. This vile attack was carried out with complete disregard of the rules governing submarine warfare as laid down in the London Naval Treaty of 1930, to which Germany was legally bound. The Treaty expressly stated that no merchant ship must be sunk without warning or until proper provision had been made for the safety of passengers and crew. But the Nazis recognised no law, no code, no decency, as they made plain that Sunday evening.

Another fact was revealed by the *Athenia* sinking. Enemy U-boats had been on the spot some time before the actual beginning of hostilities, and this was supported by the news of other sinkings within the next two days in positions indicating clearly that the submarines responsible must have started from their home ports before Mr Chamberlain's declaration of war at eleven-fifteen on the morning of the 3rd.

Heavier units, too, were out. In August the two pocket battleships *Deutschland* and *Graf Spee* had left Germany in preparation for attacks on British merchant shipping. The former was to operate in the western North Atlantic, and the latter, the ship that two years before had ridden at anchor with the British Fleet off Spithead, was to make for the rich hunting grounds of the South Atlantic. A number of U-boats had also sailed in August and at least six of them were known to be in the Western Approaches by the time war broke out.

One of these was the *Kelly*'s attacker. The incident of the U-boat had sobered some of the more carefree spirits aboard. The enemy had, as Captain Mountbatten had forewarned, lost no time in trying to destroy them. Luckily they were still afloat to tell the tale and had even taken their revenge on their enemy, as far as that could be known. But the situation might easily have been reversed and a brand-new Fleet destroyer lost on only the second day of war. The fire-eaters who had taken it for granted that a ship with half a 'probable' to her credit had practically won the war were reminded forcibly that the ship was still on her working-up trials. She was not yet fit to join the Fleet, and Captain Mountbatten had no intention of showing her bows to the enemy until he was thoroughly satisfied that her fighting efficiency was well up to standard.

The *Kelly* was certainly on her way towards being a 'happy' ship, but she was not yet an 'efficient' one.

CHAPTER IV

TWILIGHT WAR

WEYMOUTH BAY seemed to have been cleared of U-boats. At any rate, try as they might, the *Kelly*'s ship's company could not call up any more monsters from those blue shallows. Lookouts strained their eyes until they almost popped from their sockets, stokers off watch came up and stood on the hot iron deck by the funnel, glaring belligerently at the waves, as if so scare a periscope up into depth-charge range. As they did so their mouths watered. Buckets and attached heaving-lines were kept at the ready, and Posty could not be parted from his gaff. But there were no fish of any kind for the present.

By now everyone had begun to settle in and establish a routine for himself. 'Pilot' Butler-Bowdon practically lived in the charthouse. His messmates soon found that it was almost impossible to drag him away from his charts and books, and for weeks on end he would sleep on a camp bed amongst them without going near his cabin. On at least one occasion the Captain had to order him to leave the ship and go home on leave.

'Guns', Alistair Robin, as a Scot, a big-boned, fair-haired man with an aggressive jaw and a look of the ascetic about him. 'Guns' moods seemed always to run contrary to events. When nothing at all was happening he would appear excitable. In action or in a tight corner, on the other hand, the action seemed to satisfy him and he was a model of coolness.

The vital period of working up was all too short for the efficiency of the ship, but there was a war on and the new destroyers would have to be thrown into the battle as soon as they were in the mimimum state of readiness. But if the Portland trials were too short for Admiralty standards, they were all too long for the men of the *Kelly*. It is no romantic moonshine to say that they all wanted some action, especially as their appetites had been whetted by that early taste of blood. All around them the counters of war were being moved into place. The convoy system was in action and other destroyers were out hunting U-boats. The British Expeditionary Force had begun to move across into France, and at home air-raid precautions were coming into force. Everyone, in fact, was getting on with the war except the *Kelly*, and it was about time she had a good look at the enemy.

Mountbatten felt this deeply. He, like his First Lord at the Admiralty, believed in attack. 'Go hard for your man,' he had written in his *Introduction to Polo*. Both on the polo field and at sea his motto, which was now that of the ship he commanded, was 'Keep On'. He believed in getting in the first blow, and he burned to put this belief into practice.

He believed even more in being ready, in training for the fight. 'The morale of your team is of paramount importance,' was another maxim from his polo handbook which revealed the man. The morale of this team was already high.

It was high because everyone now realised that they could count on a square deal from the Captain. True, he worked them hard, but he worked twice as hard himself. He cracked the whip a bit at times, but he never gave them the green rub.

Of course there were one or two who wouldn't play. Skates and sea-lawyers never die. But they cut no ice aboard the *Kelly*. The Captain made it quite clear that he would have no mercy on anyone who let the ship down.

On September 12th the *Kelly* left Portland and headed for the Channel. They were on what was supposed to be a secret mission, but very few 'secret missions' ever beat the buzz, and the object of this one was common knowledge some time before they sailed.

During the week Captain Mountbatten had been called to the Admiralty. On the Saturday someone read in the *Daily Mirror* that one of Britain's fastest and newest destroyers had been selected to go over to France and bring the Duke and Duchess of Windsor home. Aboard the *Kelly* they put two and two together. Added to the guesswork was the recollection that the ship had been originally intended to take the King and Queen to Belgium and that some of the interior decorations of the cabins had been 'poshed up' accordingly. They wouldn't be taking a king to Belgium, but they might very well be bringing an ex-king back.

Such was the guess and it proved to be inspired. At the Admiralty Mountbatten was given secret orders to pick up a mysterious Officer X off the South Coast and make for Le Havre with all speed. On the Monday the *Kelly* received a signal from the Captain to raise full steam by eleven hundred hours to sail on a secret mission. So the ship 'flashed up' for a secret mission that was no longer a secret from her ship's company. In fact, when the Captain rejoined his ship in highly dramatic circumstances, with all but the last wires and fenders cleared away and the *Kelly*'s funnel practically red-hot as she strained at the leash, almost the first words he heard were from the First Lieutenant, who said that the ship's company had just told him that they were going to France to bring the Duke and Duchess of Windsor home. The Captain mentioned this with a rather rueful grin when he cleared lower deck and briefed them for the operation.

Then they were off, and under the shadow of cloak and dagger steamed up the coast. The mysterious officer turned out to be the First Lord's son, Randolph Churchill, who had been sent by the First Lord as his personal representative. With him safely aboard, the *Kelly* got off her mark and sprinted for Le Havre. Her stern went down and the waters parted before her. Fair stood the wind for France that day, and fairer still was the electrifying turn of speed they got out of her engines. They would have been proud of her that day, the little seven-horse-power Tyne packet, the gunboat of 1862 and the Fleet *Viper* of 1899, whose fine, though freakish speed the *Kelly* now surpassed. It was the first time she had gone flat out, and she was a splendid advertisement for her builders as she made the pace across the narrow sea.

'By gum,' said one man, 'she can leg it an' all!'

'Aye,' said a leading hand, 'an' if she goes on bashing away like this she'll burst a bleedin' blood vessel.'

At Le Havre Major Churchill went ashore and escorted the Duke and Duchess back to the ship. Once aboard, the Duke shook hands with all the officers and inspected the ship's company. Bert Male had seen the Duke before, when he was King, and he had noticed then how tired and worn he had looked, with the burden of a disturbed and uncertain kingship upon his shoulders. But now, shorn of a heavy crown, the head no longer lay uneasy. In spite of their long and tiring car journey across France, dodging the heavy streams of military traffic, both the Duke and Duchess looked well, and the Duke himself seemed years younger. After the inspection they went below, and the Duke enjoyed a quiet family dinner with his cousin in the Captain's cabin.

Meanwhile the *Kelly* had kicked up her heels again. The urgency of the occasion was doubled now and she was driven even harder this time. Germany had the best part of sixty submarines positioned round the British Isles. Some of these were in the Channel area, and if any of them had found out what a valuable cargo the *Kelly* was carrying that day, how could they resist the temptation? But apparently they did not know. Perhaps they did not read the *Daily Mirror*. A submarine did, however, shadow the ship on the way back. The port for'ard lookout reported a periscope a full half-hour after he had first sighted it. When the Captain had finished with that man he wanted to crawl away and find a big hole in the Channel to hide his shame in. But the submarine did not attack, and the trip was otherwise uneventful. Rogers left the messdeck and took a turn on deck in the cool evening air. The night was very dark and still. He stood on the fo'c'sle, leaning against the guard-rails just below 'B' gundeck and looked at the calm sea and the white flurry of the bow-wave. He clasped his hands tightly on the rail and felt the great throb of power in the ship as she fled over the water to Portsmouth.

When they arrived they came alongside at Farewell Jetty. They drew alongside the jetty in silence. Then someone switched on a single overhead light ashore and they could see a small reception committee waiting, with a big closed car in the background. As the Duke and Duchess came down from the bridge the gangway lights were switched on. They shone on the bayonets of the guard of honour lined up ashore. When the time came to leave, the *Kelly*'s guests stepped off the quarterdeck and went slowly down the gangway. Half-way down they turned back towards the men lined up along the rail, and each of them in turn wished the *Kelly*'s ship's company God speed in the months that lay ahead. The men returned the compliment by giving them a loud and prolonged cheer. The cheering rang across the darkened jetty; then, as the Duke reached the bottom of the gangway, it faltered, became ragged and died away as the fullness of the scene became felt by all. The Duke seemed to hesitate for a second, then stepped off the gangway. The ex-King of England had touched his native soil again for the first time in three years of exile. An incident which had begun almost as melodrama now touched the memory of tragedy.

After the V.I.P.s had been disembarked, leave was piped for all *bona fide* natives until midnight. Nobby Clarke and a few of his oppos from the P.O.s' mess reported at the gangway and, after telling the Coxswain that they were natives of any port in the world, went ashore and made for the nearest tavern and a little lemonade. Those left aboard got some much-needed sleep. But all hands were called early next morning, when the *Kelly* left Pompey and made for Plymouth.

Plymouth is a place where the wind blows free. Over the dockyard from Drake's Island comes the salt breeze of England's first greatness as a sea power, ruffling the Sound, sending its freshness over the Hoe and down the streets into the town, having in it the crackle of burning treasure ships, the flapping pennants of the *Golden Hind* and the muffled thunder of Drake's drum, blowing hope and the salt tang of freedom from the wide expanses of sea and sky.

It even improves life in the Royal Navy Barracks at Devonport, close by. There, the narrow roadways lead down between the mess blocks to the bright harbour edged with the black geometry of cranes and the grey hulls of warships. Life is much the same as in Chatham or Pompey, except that nothing seems to matter quite so much in Guz. It is as if spring were always in the air there, a sort of 'Christmas Day in the workhouse' feeling all the time. You may be coaling party, or on draft routine, or in the rattle, or in trouble with your party's father, but there are always tiddley oggies in the canteen and that lovely dogfish and duff for dinner, and there's always the Jenny-Wrens, though most of them are only waiting for the gold braid to come alongside and won't look at a poor matelot. This is the place of which Charles Causley, himself an ex-Guz rating, writes:

Myself, on the long winter evenings,
  I find myself thinking of the Royal Naval Barracks
    at Devonport:
Remembering the jolly stokers, the yellow-faced
  Dark-haired sick-bay tiffies, the Mongolian Chief-
    Yeomen,
And, behind the backcloth of cranes and acetylene
  welders,
  The splendid sea.

But the men of the *Kelly* were not likely to see much of R.N.B., Devonport, and they wouldn't have thanked you for the chance. Provided she's a good ship, life afloat is always infinitely sweeter than being a barrack stanchion. But they would be glad of a tour of the town, a plate of eggs and chips and a couple of hours in the boozer or a date with a little party (her knocking back gin and limes and you making one beer last the evening). There might even be a crafty trip to the Snake Pit if there wasn't a patrol about.

They passed Drake's Island on September 13th and entered harbour. That night they had their first run ashore in Plymouth and found the atmosphere ashore a trifle jumpy.

It was the same all over the country. After the announcement of war on the third of the month a general feeling of tension and nervous excitement mounted swiftly. Sandbagged anti-blast walls and air-raid shelters could be seen being rapidly constructed. Gas-masks were being issued, and some of the more fearful fully expected air-raids to begin any day upon London. At sea it seemed as if Germany were carrying on the U-boat game just where she had left off in 1918, and once again the thought of starvation by submarine threw the minds of some of the older generation into gloom and despondency. When the days passed and no spectacular disaster fell upon them the people began to relax again and the tension eased. Those who wondered why Hitler did not strike were consoled by the optimists who said that he held his hand only because it was too occupied in knocking the life out of Poland.

It was certainly true, and the more enquiring minds could read the tragic story in their newspapers, that the country we had pledged ourselves to support was fighting a grim and bloody battle alone against the Germans. On September 1st a savage blitzkrieg was let loose on Poland. The Polish armies stood up to it manfully and fought desperately for their homeland, but were driven back steadily by the armoured fury of the Wehrmacht and the lewd butchery of the Luftwaffe, who bombed and machine-gunned every man, woman and child, every naked city they could see, like cut-throat bandits gone crazy in a sea of loot. Armies were broken and their remnants wiped out in a general slaughter. On the day the *Kelly* brought the Duke and Duchess of Windsor to Portsmouth the Nazi Fourteenth Army had reached Lemberg in the eastern extremity of Poland and had begun to drive north towards the advancing Third Army which had thrust down from East Prussia. In between those iron jaws Poland expired in agony.

But even Hitler had to have a breathing space, a chance to look at his map and size up the situation, a time to regroup and reposition his forces for the great offensive against Britain and France. The end of Poland came swiftly. On the 17th the Fourteenth and Third Armies joined and the trap was closed. Within its arms all remaining Polish forces were cut to pieces and the Germans proudly announced to the world that the great battle of the Vistula was 'one of the greatest battles of extermination of all time'.

At the same time Russia had come into the dirty game. When all organised Polish resistance was clearly seen to be over, Russian armies invaded Poland from the east and advanced towards the Germans. The two 'allies' met at Bret Litovsk, scene of the capitulation of the Red Army to the Kaiser in the First World War, and exchanged wary smiles over a handshake. Poland was parcelled out between the two rapists, and Communist and Nazi settled down to watch each other across the new frontier. Now Hitler could turn his attention to the Western Front. Now he would switch those fifty-six divisions that had crushed Poland and throw them against the French Army and the four divisions of the British Expeditionary Force.

But weeks, then months passed and he continued to disappoint the armchair generals. It was not until March of the next year that he made his next big move.

The months between were strained and anxious. Smart Alecks in America called this period 'the phoney war'. Mr Churchill has given it the happier title of 'the twilight war'.

For Britain it was indeed a period of twilight – or, rather, of the cold, grey hour before dawn. For us there were no vast-scale movements, no great victories or shocking debacles during that time. In that twilight, in that vague mist of shifting shadows and shapeless uncertainties and apprehensions, only isolated events showed up as realities. A string of victories and disasters flared up at intervals like solitary explosions breaking the darkness of a long, uneasy night. Most of them happened at sea, and were all flowers of the stealthy sowing the Germany Navy had done before war broke out.

By the time the *Kelly* had arrived at Plymouth the convoy system was in operation. Outward-bound sailings had been arranged and ships were routed along three different paths: one from Liverpool into the Atlantic, one from the Thames down the Channel and past the Bishop Rock into the western Atlantic, and one along the East Coast between the Thames and the Forth. At the same time the routing of homeward-bound convoys from Halifax, Gibraltar and Freetown was being organised. Where the convoys steamed the U-boats would be sure to gather, and the *Kelly* went out on several patrols from Plymouth in her first few days there.

With the convoy system operating, the lack of destroyers and escort vessels really became felt. Plans for a vast increase in the number of anti-submarine vessels were being implemented with all possible speed. All long-term naval programmes were scrapped and every effort was concentrated on the manufacture of weapons to meet the present emergency. Large numbers of 'utility' destroyers were to be built, ships that could be constructed, launched and put into service in less than twelve months. Eighty-six of the largest and fastest trawlers were in the process of being equipped with Asdics so that they could go on convoy duty almost immediately. Guns could be fitted at a later stage. In addition to these ships many new vessels of a type called 'corvettes' were being built.

However, before the Asdic trawlers came into service there would be a gap of two or three weeks. To bridge this gap it would be necessary to run the existing destroyer strength ragged, both in anti-submarine patrolling and in convoy escort work, great reliance being placed on their Asdics. Destroyers were taken from the Home Fleet and given to the convoys. Even then the escorts were all too few in number and the merchant ships lost their services once they had reached a line 20° 30′ West. This line stretched round the western fringe of the British Isles, only eighty miles west of Ireland and two hundred and thirty miles west of the Scillies.

One of the reasons for this restriction in the arc of operations of the over-worked destroyers was the immediate loss of the southern Irish ports at the outbreak of war. Our ships could not use these ports to operate against submarines, but, on the other hand, it did not require much imagination to picture these same submarines refuelling in rocky caves and inlets on the Irish coast. But that was just one more cross to bear. Luckily the Navy's back is strong.

Another measure taken to fill the gap was very much in the nature of a calculated risk. Foreshadowing the later 'killer' group, comprising an escort carrier and attendant anti-submarine vessels, and Admiralty decided to use the big Fleet carriers in conjunction with destroyer escorts. Strung out over the Atlantic, so many sitting ducks for the U-boats, were many merchant ships 'caught with their pants down' when war broke out. All these were now approaching our ports unprotected from torpedo attack. The carrier groups were to help these unfortunates home.

A northern group very soon drew blood. On September 14th the *Ark Royal*, with the escorting destroyer *Faulkner*, *Foxhound* and *Firedrake*, was patrolling one hundred and fifty miles west of the Hebrides, when the U39 made a torpedo attack on her. The torpedoes missed and the destroyers attacked. The depth-charges found their mark and U39 was blown to the surface.

All ships outward-bound in the Channel and Irish Sea at the outbreak of war had been ordered to Plymouth or Milford Haven. It was to help these as well as the homeward-bound ships that the *Kelly* and her sisters were at Plymouth. The *Kelly* did her share of escort duty in those first days and steamed through some heavy weather in the course of her job as nursemaid.

One night, in very dirty weather, they were investigating a possible submarine contact off Land's End when an S O S came into the wireless office. It was from the aircraft- carrier *Courageous*, which had been patrolling the South-western Approaches in her role as stop-gap anti-submarine measure. She had been steaming in the approaches to the Bristol Channel on the evening of the 17th with her escort of four destroyers. A patrol of her Swordfish aircraft was up and about due to land on again, when two of her escorts had to be detached to hunt a U-boat that was attacking a merchant ship. Thus, at dusk, when she turned into wind to take her aircraft aboard, she was without her full escort at a time when an aircraft-carrier is at her most vulnerable. By a supremely unlucky chance the time and the place and the U-boat coincided. Two torpedoes struck her and she began to sink. As soon as her S O S had gone out all ships in the vicinity raced to her assistance. When it was picked up aboard the *Kelly* she raised all steam and went flat out towards the carrier's reported position.

Down below in the engine-room Rogers had the first watch, from eight o'clock until midnight. Suddenly the engine-room telegraph rang Full Ahead and away they went. They steamed through choppy water and every wave that struck the hull sent a shudder through her that could be felt throughout the ship.

Nobby Clarke felt it on deck. He had never moved so fast over water before. It was a dark night, and as they neared the estimated position, about an hour after they had first received the S O S, Nobby was sent for'ard into the bows to see of he could spot any wreckage as they steamed along. It was all he could do to hang on in the bows at that speed, but he stuck there and very soon saw lights ahead.

The lights were not, as some of the men on the *Kelly*'s upper deck at first thought, fires raging aboard the *Courageous.* The carrier had gone down by then and the lights blazed from two neutral liners, an American and a Dutchman, that had come up to rescue survivors. There were several other British destroyers there, all in darkness in case the U-boat that had sunk the aircraft-carrier should be still in the vicinity. The *Courageous* had carried a crew of one thousand two hundred and sixty, over five hundred of whom were lost, including her Captain. Of those who had survived the explosions and managed to take to the water many had choked to death in the icy sea and the filthy morass of oil fuel and aviation spirit that covered the area around the sunken ship and stank in the nostrils of the rescuers. The *Kelly* steamed over the area and picked up a few men. One of these was the Commander of the *Courageous*, Commander Abel Smith, now the Vice-Admiral Commanding the Royal Yachts. He had been one of King George VI's equerries and had been released on the outbreak of war to become Chief Executive Officer of the *Courageous.*

She then went alongside the American liner and took off the forty-seven survivors that the neutral vessel had picked up from the sea. It was a very rough night, and getting alongside the American ship comfortably enough for the wounded men to be transferred directly from ship to ship soon proved to be impossible. The wind was now blowing a gale and the two ships heaved and lurched, dangerously close. The raging black sea crashed against their sides, boiling and seething at deck level as they rolled, racing away with the *Kelly's* heaving lines, which were all flung back by the wind and fell short. They tried another way. The *Kelly* drew off and lowered the motor cutter into that murderous sea. Slowly they fought their way across to the liner's towering side. There, after many unsuccessful attempts, they got a line aboard her and started to take the first batch of sick and wounded men down over the side and safely into the tiny cabin of the motor cutter. They took them singly, slowly and with infinite patience. These were their mates, their fellow-matelots, savaged and shocked by a brutal enemy. The crew of the cutter had their hands full that desperate night, between helping the injured men and fending off from the slimy metal mass that swayed above them, threatening at any moment to crush the timbers of the little boat and grind them and their helpless passengers into the sea. That sea was icy as it broke inboard, and the wind knifed through their sodden clothing to the bone. On the second trip a rope fouled the screw. The officer in charge of the boat and his leading seaman went over the side in the darkness and cut it away. Then the whole trembling business began again. Finally they made their last trip back to the *Kelly* and were hoisted inboard again. They were never so glad to see the old ship before.

The *Kelly* searched the area of the sinking for two hours before she left for Devonport to land the survivors. In the sick bay Bert Male attended to the men they had dragged from the sea. He made them as comfortable as possible, but they were all exhausted and suffering from shock, burns and lacerations. One man, a stoker, was carried below to Roger's mess. This man had slid down the ship's side when she heeled over. The barnacles had torn his back, buttocks and hands and he was in a very bad way. The gash bucket in the mess was full of tealeaves and scrapings off the supper plates. When he saw the bucket the survivor fell to his knees and plunged his lacerated and bloody hands right into it.

'Don't do that, old matey,' said Gordon, and tried to hold him back; 'you'll get blood poisoning or something.'

'I don't give a damn,' he said. 'It's cool, cool, cool!'

When he looked closer, Rogers saw that the man was drunk. The well-meaning Americans had poured a whole bottle of whisky into him. But drink was not all they had given the exhausted men. All those that were taken aboard the *Kelly* came wrapped in thick blankets and warm clothes. Many of the survivors were worried about the state of the money they had had in the pouches of their belts, and the ship's cooks were busy throughout the night drying out pound notes on the top of the range.

On her way back to port with the survivors the *Kelly* received a signal giving the position of a newly torpedoed ship. As none of the survivors' condition was considered dangerous, she steamed at full speed to the spot and started searching. They hunted all night, and on the 19th carried out depth-charge attacks. After the attacks the *Kelly* steamed back over the area. They saw some oil, and a few pieces of wreckage came to the surface, but it was an unsatisfying conclusion to the tragedy of the night before. It was thought afterwards that some of the wreckage had come from the sunken ship, the *Accrington Court*, which had remained air-locked at a certain depth and was moving along in the current.

However, they had one small consolation in the fact that the depth-charge explosions had stunned a large shoal of sea bream, and very soon, with the aid of buckets and other handy items, the upper deck was turned into a floating fishmonger's shop. They took care to see that the best of the catch went to the survivors, who rapidly improved under the treatment they received on board. When the ship came alongside ambulances were waiting to take the *Courageous* men to hospital. The *Kelly*'s ship's company were fully occupied throwing fish to the dockyard mateys. They had had their fill, and the Buffer was glad to see his upper deck clean again. Nobby Clarke had just got rid of the last bucketful when a messenger came up to him from aft to beg some fish for the Captain of the Dockyard.

'Sorry, mate,' said Nobby. 'Just report back and tell him his dockyard mateys have pinched the lot.'

Knight still persevered with the *K.D.F. News*, and next day's issue, No. 26, commented on the ship's programme.

THE KELLY – TODAY'S PROGRAMME.

> The *Kelly* sails at 0730 today to escort the *Hermes* out of harbour while she is operating her aircraft. On completion of flying exercises the *Hermes* returns to Plymouth and the *Kelly* proceeds to Portland to join the *Kingston* for her working-up practices.

This paragraph tells us the significant fact that the *Kelly* now had a consort. There were now two ships in the Fighting Fifth. But the new girl, *Kingston,* still had to do her working-up trials, and *Kelly* was to lead her through them by the hand, at the same time getting in some more valuable practice herself. Knight's column went on,

THE KINGSTON'S PROGRAMME.

> According to present arrangements the *Kingston* should be carrying out her torpedo discharge trials at Portland today. A meeting will be held on board the *Kelly,* attended by the *Kingston's* officers, at which details of her working-up programme will be prepared. The object of Captain (D)'s staff will be to lend the *Kingston* every assistance in getting worked-up as quickly as possible. The *Kelly* will be accompanying the *Kingston* to sea most of the time, not only to help her, but because this gives the *Kelly* a wonderful opportunity to consolidate her own working-up which none can deny was rather 'over-rushed', particularly coming on top of the mad scramble of commissioning.

Under the heading 'THE KELLY – YESTERDAY'S EVENTS', the paper had this to say about the U-boat hunt which followed the picking up of the *Courageous* survivors:

> An all-night search and hunt culminated in depth-charge attacks, which produced oil, pillows and a lavatory door. Although members of the Submarine Service assure us that submarines are fitted with every modern convenience, the shape of the door was such as to make it more likely to have come from the wreck of the torpedoed ship.

It was a grim joke, in the circumstances, but only those not actively engaged in a war can afford to take its grimmer horrors too seriously.

CHAPTER V

SEA-TIME

For the next month the *Kelly* remained at Plymouth. During that time she made many sorties, hunting U-boats and escorting convoys up and down the Channel. They must have worried the life out of any U-boats that were stationed in the area, waiting for easy pickings. Egg Burnett and his men were kept busy, and the Asdics were singing night and day. They depth-charged many a wretched bunch of Nazis locked in their steel coffins down in the shell-shocked darkness of green fathoms. Although they scored no certain 'kill', they damaged several U-boats and threw others out of their stride, saving many ships from the fate of the *Courageous* and the *Accrington Court.*

Kelly seemed to be always on call for a U-boat hunt. Even the *Kingston*'s working-up trials had to be interrupted. On the second day of the programme the *Kelly* was despatched to the position of a sinking merchant ship. This was another *'Court'*, the *Kensington Court*. When the *Kelly* got there, with all her rivets jumping in their holes, the cupboard was bare alike of ship, U-boats and survivors. The thirty-four members of the *Kingston Court*'s crew had already been picked up by Royal Air Force Sunderland flying-boats and brought to England. Here was a new development – the rescue of a sunken ship's crew by air.

The *Kelly*'s dramatic departures from harbour on the track of U-boats became so famous in Plymouth that the dockyard thought the war had ended if she came alongside for an 'all-night-in'. On one occasion, when she flashed up in a hurry and cast off wires and fenders at the double, a dockyard matey who was standing by her wires said, ' 'ere we go again; those mad bastards 'ave scented blood. They ought to call 'er "U-boat Kelly".' And after a few more sorties everyone did. If there was a U-boat about the *Kelly* was always to windward of her.

Things got so lively that the watch could hardly go ashore for more than a few minutes before they were dragged back again for some more sea-time.

'It doesn't matter where you go, to the pictures or a pub or what,' read Rogers Senior, back in the little shop at Sefton Park. 'You haven't been in there more than half a dog-watch when you get the recall and away you go laughing, chasing another boatload of Jerry bandits.'

One day they were escorting a convoy up the Channel, when one of the ships was hit by a torpedo. Immediately the escorting warships made for the area where the U-boat was likely to be, the *Kelly* well to the fore. Soon they got a ping and commenced depth-charging over the position of the contact. After the second pattern a huge flower of oil blossomed on the surface and a few moments later the bows of a submarine broke surface in a gush of foam and fuel, blown to the top by the explosions. The *Kelly*'s gun crews stood by to give it hell. Then, as suddenly as she had appeared, the bows of the U-boat canted to an even sharper angle and she slid back into the depths of the sea.

'One up for us,' said Nobby Clarke. 'We must have hit the sod.'

'Poor bastards,' said Rogers, up on deck for a breath of air.

'Good riddance to bad rubbish, you mean,' said Nobby, who had the right of it.

After their victim had gone to the bottom, the *Kelly* remained in the area for a time to make sure that the submarine stayed where she had been put. She is still on the bottom today.

When the ship got back to Plymouth a party of *Kelly* men met their favourite dockyard matey, the one who was so handy at coining nicknames for their ship.

'Well, and 'ow's the Asdic Express today?' he asked.

'All right, thanks, mate,' said Nobby. 'Ran over a U-boat yesterday.'

The sight of that U-boat had been a tonic, though everyone had had about enough of Western Approaches for a while. However, they did not have very long to drip about it, because on October 20th they left Plymouth. The centre of the naval war had shifted to northern waters and where grand strategy called the newest units of the Fleet had to follow.

For a long time now the traditional base of the Home Fleet had been Scapa Flow, the great ocean-lake formed by the rocky walls of the Mainland, South Ronaldsay and Hoy in the Orkney Islands. From here the eyes of the Commander-in-Chief could cover the wide green plains of the northern oceans, from the great deeps of the North Atlantic in the west, round through the point where Iceland touches the Arctic Circle to the frozen North Cape of Norway, and down to his own special parish of the North Sea. In the First World War, Jellicoe and Beatty had kept their great dreadnoughts there and from this landlocked fortress had steamed out and driven the German Navy off the seas.

At the outbreak of this new conflict it was of immediate importance to decide on a main base for the Home Fleet. Two days after war was declared the new First Lord of the Admiralty held a conference to decide the matter. As an outcome of the conference Scapa Flow was once more chosen as the Fleet's home. For one thing, out of all possible choices for a base, Scapa was the farthest from German air bases, particularly from those of torpedo-carrying aircraft. It was argued by some that the Firth of Forth would give the Fleet a better chance of intercepting units of the German fleet as they put out from their home ports. The more pressing problems of air defences could be simplified by the Firth sharing the air defences of the Scottish industrial areas. But Scapa was better situated for the control of all northern waters in general and in particular for the enforcement of the northern blockade of Germany and the prevention of German warships from breaking out into the North Atlantic by sailing north of the Orkneys.

So Scapa it was to be.

Mr Churchill went there on September 14th and spent several days inspecting the defences. These he had already judged inadequate, in view of the new threats from modern submarines and from aircraft, but he was assured that they were 'as good as in the last war', and that improvements agreed upon at the conference of September 5th were in the process of being made.

The defences of Scapa had not kept in step with modern methods of attack. Anti-submarine defences had been provided only on the scale adequate for an occasional re-fuelling base. Anti-aircraft defences were slender, only a handful of guns defending the naval oil tanks at Hoy and the destroyer anchorage, although the Admiralty had promised to provide two fighter squadrons, to be stationed at Kirkwall, on the Mainland to the north of Scapa, whenever the Fleet was in the Flow.

Because Scapa Flow had remained immune from attack throughout the 1914–18 war, complacency ruled it impregnable in 1939. It seemed to have been forgotten that no one who used the Flow in the earlier war ever felt quite safe there, even then, and that there had, in fact, been several U-boat scares which had sent the Grand Fleet hurriedly to sea.

Such complacency was riding for a fall, and the disaster was not long in coming. On the very day when the *Kelly* was at Dover attacking her U-boat another U-boat got into Scapa Flow and sank the battleship *Royal Oak*.

This operation had been carefully planned by Admiral Doenitz himself, then Flag Officer (Submarines). As Lieutenant Prien, in U47, arrived off the eastern approaches to the Flow and began investigating Holm Sound, he discovered a gap between the blockships in Kirk Sound to the north. Once through that gap he was in Scapa Flow. He found his prize lying at anchor in the northern end of the anchorage and fired two salvoes of torpedoes into her. She sank with the loss of nearly eight hundred officers and men and Prien went back the way he had come. Twenty-four hours later a blockship arrived.

Those ships that were in the Flow were immediately dispersed to other harbours. The Germans anticipated that the Fleet would be sent to the Firth of Forth and bombed that place on the 16th. The cruisers *Southampton* and *Edinburgh* were hit, and twenty-five men were killed on the destroyer *Mohawk*. But the raid was not a paying proposition, and the loss of half the German bombing force made it less so. The day after the raid on the Forth bombers attacked Scapa, and the old battleship *Iron Duke*, Jellicoe's flagship in the Grand Fleet, was hit and settled on the bottom.

As the result of U47's coup Scapa Flow was put out of action as a main Fleet base for six months, while radical improvements were made in its defences. It was still maintained as a destroyer refuelling base, but meanwhile temporary accommodation had to be found for the big ships.

On this point the experts differed. The Admiralty favoured the Clyde, but the Commander-in-Chief, Home Fleet, pointed out that this would mean an extra day's steaming each way to his operational area, besides the provision of extra escorting destroyers and the necessity for him to weaken his main force by splitting it into the two divisions necessary to cover two fronts. Eventually Rosyth was chosen as the temporary 'main operational base of the Fleet', being more suitable geographically, though more vulnerable to air attack. Improvements in its defences were ordered at once. Meanwhile, the Home Fleet would have to used the Clyde, badly positioned though they would be, to catch any German raiders breaking out to the north, while some ships would be kept on the East Coast. Auxiliary to the establishment of a main base, use was to be made of a number of other anchorages around the Scottish coast. One of the best of these was Loch Ewe, on the west coast of Ross and Cromarty facing the Hebrides across the Channel called The Minch. This anchorage was thought to be almost immune from air attack and would, at least, be slightly better placed for the job of interception. This was the 'Port A' of the First Lord's despatch to D.C.N.S. on November 1st, which ran as follows:

> Port A is to be maintained in its present position with its existing staff. A permanent boom and net is to be provided even before the Scapa nets are completed. The freshwater pipe is to be finished and any minor measures taken to render this base convenient as a concealed resting-place for the Fleet from time to time.

To this 'concealed resting-place', on October 21st, 1939, came the *Kelly*. She steamed slowly through the narrow, rocky entrance into the cold loch and joined her new companions and brothers in exile under the shadow of the towering, purple hills. She was to know Loch Ewe better in the months to come, though this, her first visit, was to be a brief one. Having left her card, she steamed out again a few days later. Out into The Minch she glided, and, with a smart turn to starboard, followed the fifty-fathom line northwards. Stornaway was left away to port, Broad Bay and the Butt of Lewis, then starboard again to round Cape Wrath and set her course for lonely Scapa. Following the shifting scene of war, the *Kelly* had done her first Grand Tour of Britain, from the fairer south to the cold north, from Land's End literally to John O'Groats. As they steamed through Switha Sound, the 'tradesman's entrance' to the Flow, the Officer of the Watch turned to the duty signalman.

'Know what day it is?' he asked.

Of course I know what ruddy day it is, thought the signalman, and if you're going to make a crack about there being fireworks ahead I'm for a draft chit to big ships here and now.

Guy Fawkes' Day was cold, and bleak, and miserable. The special sea-dutymen closed up in their oilskins and the cable party up for'ard slipped and slithered on the wet fo'c'sle in a wretched scrap-heap of Blake slips, hosepipes and banging, berserk cable. They dropped the hook and went below, dripping in all senses, wishing they had joined the army. Another chapter in their lives had begun, a six-month tour in the brief, uncertain daylight and grey seas of the Arctic battleground.

Scapa, they found, was a tender spot in the Navy's anatomy. It was a long time before the shock of the *Royal Oak* sinking subsided. In fact the buzz ran that the *Kelly* had been sent north expressly to catch Prien and his U47, and many of them half expected to see him again at any moment, in spite of the new blockships and anti-submarine nets. At any rate, it didn't take much to set the alarm bells ringing. 'Every floating broomstick is a periscope up here,' wrote Bob Knight. The job of 'duty destroyer' quickly ceased to have any meaning, because every ship was on duty all the time. During those bitter six months they were to plough most of the cheerless acres of salt between Greenland and Norway. In the course of their weary routine of patrols they got in enough genuine sea-time to last them for the rest of their lives. They were at everyone's beck and call for whatever dirty or dangerous job happened to land on the plate of the small ships.

Of course they were intensely proud of being a small ship. In the Navy there are two kinds of men: big-ship sailors and small-ship sailors. A matelot will describe himself as 'Big ships, me', or, usually with a great deal more pride 'Small ships, myself'. Big ships have their partisans, of course – timid, gregarious souls who seem to find comfort in numbers. But to the gypsies, the pirates, the small-ship men, a capital ship is only a gangway's length from the purgatory of barracks. It is a limbo of brass and bull and bugles, a great metal pile that 'heaps a skyscraper over the breathing ribs'. When you hear a man describe himself as 'big ships' you can usually detect a note of apology in his voice. He has probably picked this up from too many encounters with scornful swashbucklers from destroyers, corvettes or M.T.B.s who have sooner or later accused him of having spent more days swinging round the buoy than they've had hot dinners.

But there wasn't any swinging round the buoy for the big ships of the Home Fleet. Two German pocket battleships were out somewhere on the trade routes, and any of those long, Arctic nights might see other ocean raiders try to slip into the Atlantic through the northern escape hatch. They were on the perpetual alert and spent almost as much time at sea as the destroyers.

The *Kelly* could bear witness to that. She made many long trips escorting the big ships up into the Arctic Circle, looking for trouble.

Rogers had thought himself an old sea-dog by now, but one earlier excursion round Iceland in company with the *Hood* showed him up. The weather was about as different as it could be from the gentle calm of that moonlit night when the *Kelly* had glided over the water from Pompey to Plymouth. Nothing 'glided' up here except the sea-gulls, who did some effective dive-bombing when Gordon heaved his heart up in the Denmark Straits.

'What's that flipping land over there?' he asked, with a feeble attempt at being Jack-my-Hearty in between spells of skite-hawk feeding.

'That's *Green*land, mate,' said an unfeeling voice; '*Green*, to match your face, me old wingsybash. Would you like a plate of cowboy – nice cold, congealed bacon and beans? They got some left in the galley. . . .'

The *Kelly* men got to know the *Hood* quite well. One or two even tried to get a draft to her.

'Just the job for me,' said one man; 'keep you dry when it's raining.'

There was a great deal of truth in that remark, truth that was bitter for the destroyer men. Much of their affection for the battle-cruiser could be traced to a sort of cupboard love – unfortunately unrequited. It was all right back in port or up the line with the party. Then it would become a fine thing to be in a destroyer – glamorous, heroic, tough. But here, in the Arctic, with every wave breaking inboard and every stitch they possessed sodden wet with icy spray, they envied the men aboard the big ships and forgot all about the bugles.

For they were in no way equipped for the Arctic conditions. At that time there was no heating on the mess-decks and no warm clothing. The woollen comforts would come later, when the loving mothers of Hostilities Only ratings sent their little parcels of balaclavas, mittens and scarves to the shivering men of the Home Fleet. About the only thing they had to keep out the cold was the rum. To open their numbed and ice-bound arteries, Mountbatten's men dosed themselves with Nelson's Blood. A tot was a life-saver, and many a 'Temperance' rating changed his mind under the pressure of cold wet bones and a freezing belly. There were no sippers to be had for love nor money and few tots were bottled.

For clothing they had to improvise. Anti-flash gear, overcoats, overalls, oilskins, sea-boots and many shifts of underclothing fought in vain against breaking sea and freezing headwinds. Many wore socks on their hands and wrapped towels round their heads. Lifelines were kept permanently rigged on deck, and if you happened to take your hand away just as a big sea smacked the ship – well, at least you wouldn't live long in that kind of water.

On the messdecks the deckhead was permanently dripping with condensation, and sea-water poured down the ammunition hoists, so that their kit was always swimming in two or three inches of water in their lockers. It was then that they envied their opposite numbers in the big ships. Every roll brought something else crashing to the deck. Most of the crockery was smashed on their first trip in heavy weather, and any luxury goods they happened to have accumulated were the first things to disintegrate under the attack of the elements. Books lost their pristine form and became pulpy, sodden splodges. Photographs of girl-friends either got hopelessly waterlogged or stuck to each other, so that faithful Doris's honest features got all mixed up with the bold face of that little tart you picked up at a dance. Everything suffered a sea-change – into something sick, wet, icy cold and weary. You couldn't keep your feet and you couldn't keep your food.

But you mustn't be downhearted.

'Shouldn't have joined if I can't take a joke,' you said.

You lurched and vomited your way through the miserable round of watchkeeping and more watchkeeping, of turning out at midnight to keep the middle on a gale-swept bridge and clawing your way down the bucking ladders again at four, to sleep like a dead log till the bell went for the next punishing spasm. Every time you got to the bridge the man you relieved said, 'Lovely weather for your dandruff.' Every time you were relieved yourself and slithered down the ladder at the break of the fo'c'sle, you fell over the seaboat's crew, huddled down there in the lee of the bridge in streaming black oilskins, looking like a Welsh choir on a Sunday. After a long, wretched, aching eternity of this you found yourself coming to the buoy again in Scapa and you didn't give a tuppenny Walls for the lot, for the P.O. of the watch, the killick of the working-party or anybody. You didn't even mind that you no longer had a decent suit to your name or a pair of good shoes.

What good was a decent suit in Scapa, anyway? What was there to go ashore for there? All you could look forward to was a pint of watery beer in what they laughingly called 'The Canteen'. This was a hut which you reached by climbing a muddy track up from the jetty. If they were lucky enough to go alongside the depot ship the Kellys could go aboard her for a change and have a game of tombola.

But if the men in the big ships were to be envied for the comparative luxury of their accommodation, theirs was no soft touch. Among the *Kelly*'s companions at this time were the ships of the Northern Patrol, the thin grey line of armed merchant-cruisers which kept the seas between Scotland and Greenland.

These frail, poorly armed ex-passenger liners, substitutes for regular units, patrolled constantly, looking for contraband and watching over any friendly merchant shipping that came within their parochial care. All German ships were captured and doubtful neutrals sent into Kirkwall for examination. This vital blockade was maintained on a line stretching from Scotland, through Iceland, to the Denmark Straits between Iceland and Greenland.

For more than a year the merchant-cruisers did their duty with unparalleled watchfulness and courage, before the situation changed sufficiently for the Northern Patrol to have outlived its usefulness.

While they were there they faced a double danger. All U-boats coming out from their homeland to work the Atlantic convoy routes passed through this northern gap, as the Channel had been made impassable for them by minefields. The merchant-cruisers lay right across their path. Again, if any of the heavy ships of the German Fleet managed to elude Admiral Forbes's battleships and battle-cruisers, and come upon one of these unarmoured, feebly armed ships, the merchant-cruiser would have no chance at all. It is not surprising that within a few months the original twenty or thirty ships had been decimated. These fine vessels and the very gallant gentlemen who served in them had to be expendable in their country's crisis. These were the men the Kellys got to know, men from ships like the *Jervis Bay* and the *Rawalpindi.*

Although the task of enforcing the contraband-control blockade in northern waters was difficult and dangerous, that of preventing the trade from northern Norway to Germany was very much more intricate and troublesome.

This trade was of greatest importance to Germany, since it consisted almost entirely of the movement of high-grade iron ore from the mines of northern Sweden. The normal route for the passage of this vital war material was from the Swedish port of Lulea, on the Gulf of Bothnia. From here the ore could be shipped, via the Baltic, to German ports. However, for nearly six months in every year Lulea was closed by ice. During those months the ore was taken overland by rail to Narvik, on the northern coast of Norway, and from there by sea down the Norwegian coast. Nearly all this voyage could be made in the shelter of territorial waters, and most of that actually under the protection of the long chain of islands that fringes Norway's coastline. These 'Inner Leads', as they were called, provided shelter that German ships exploited shamelessly.

One of the prizes taken in the Atlantic by the pocket battleship *Deutschland* in the first fortnight of October was the American ship *City of Flint*. The Germans put a prize crew aboard her and sent her home to Germany, via Norway. Information was received at the Admiralty that she was attempting to reach Kiel by steaming down the Norwegian coast under cover of the Inner Leads, and a group of destroyers, including the *Kelly* was sent to find her.

Rogers was one of those who came forward when volunteers were called for to make up a boarding party. Chronic seasickness had incapacitated the regular Royal Marine boarding party.

But the merchant ship made good use of the Norwegian territorial waters where the British warships could not follow. The *Kelly* did stray over the three-mile limit on one occasion and was cruising near the mouth of one of the fiords when a tiny gunboat appeared and threatened to open fire unless the British ship stopped her trespassing forthwith. The *Kelly* complied with the order, but not before Lord Mountbatten had shouted down to the tiny David through a megaphone, 'Please give my compliments to my cousin, Crown Prince Olaf, and tell him I hope he is keeping well.' They continued their search for the *City of Flint*, and eventually made things so uncomfortable for the captured vessel that she gave up the struggle and interned herself at Bergen.

At eight o'clock on the last morning of their search the *Kelly* received another wireless message giving the latest position of their quarry, and executed a sharp turn to press forward the chase. The weather by now had turned ugly and there was a very high and angry sea running. Just as the ship turned, and while she was still under the wheel, a tremendous sea hit her.

The force of the sea hurled the ship over and tore the wheel from the coxswain's hands. Rogers was standing just inside the galley flat on the starboard side when the ship heeled over and he was flung violently off his feet. As he picked himself up the ship slowly righted herself.

Looking aft, he saw that all the boats, davits and guard-rails on the starboard side had been torn away and the after superstructure badly battered.

Down in the stokers' mess they were having their breakfast, when, with a savage crash, the world turned upside-down. Every movable object was hurled from one side of the messdeck to the other – plates, cups, breakfast and men. Tea swilled over the deck. Two stokers sat astride a stool, holding to the mess table for dear life.

'What's that madman up to now?' shouted one above the crash of crockery.

'I don't know, but he always manages to slew when there's grub on the table,' yelled the other. 'Ride 'em cowboy!'

Bert Male was treating a patient in the sick bay when the sudden roll flung both men against the opposite bulk-head.

'I think *I* need some bloody treatment now,' he said, as he picked himself up. 'Come on, let me finish that dressing.' He had just tied the bandage, when he heard the pipe, 'All hands muster in their messes.' Outside the sick bay he bumped into the Buffer, who told him that the ship had gone over so far this time that all hands were being mustered to find out if anyone had been swept overboard. Back in the P.O.s' mess the roll was called.

They found that one man was missing – Nobby Clarke.

Immediately a search was made. They had just about come to the conclusion that poor old Nobby had been lost, when a figure staggered into the mess. His face was chalk-white, he was soaked to the skin and barefooted. The figure was just recognisable as Nobby. When he had pulled himself round again he told his story.

Nobby had been on watch on 'B' gun and had just been relieved. When he came off the gun, instead of going down to the mess through the hatch on the gundeck he decided to go aft to look for a rating who had been adrift off the morning watch. He was on the iron deck when the sea hit the ship. Nobby was knocked off his feet and buried by it. He felt a terrible sensation of bursting lungs. The next thing he knew was that he was sprawled across one of the depth-charges right at the stern, minus most of his clothes and his seaboots. He had been washed clean overboard and back again in the space of a few seconds. An hour later he was black and blue with bruises. But he was alive to tell the tale. A young stoker, who had been taking a cup of tea aft to the Engineer Officer, and was a few feet farther aft than Nobby Clarke, was not so lucky. Those few feet made all the difference, and the stoker was never seen again.

The *Kelly* fought her way back across the North Sea against continuing heavy weather. After a brief spell alongside the depot ship, the *Greenwich*, she cast off and turned south out of the Flow on her way to the Tyne.

As far as the ship's company were concerned the ship was returning to Hebburn to repair heavy-weather damage. But the real reason was Top Secret. The *Kelly*'s flotilla had been selected to carry out Operation Katherine, which called for penetration into the Baltic to attack the German Navy there. Had it come off this might have proved a 'death or glory' operation well suited to the *Kelly*. In preparation for this operation the *Kelly* was to be specially stiffened on the water-line against ice and to have general Arctic equipment fitted.

Tyneside was glad to see them. They took up where they had left off before, in those uneasy peacetime days. Soon the old Commercial rocked with yarns of war and sea-time, and many pints were stood to the now salty and seasoned matelots. At the Power House the girls had got a bit fed up with ordinary men, and when the first sailor rolled in through the door there was an excited rustle of skirts and many a fervent prayer to remember what mother had told them. And the *Kelly* men took them like conquering heroes. They were much improved from the feminine point of view. Skinny, molly-coddled civilians had filled out and toughened with the rigorous routine of destroyer life; hauling on wires and boats' falls had put muscle on flabby arms; pale faces had reddened and bronzed in the salty ocean winds.

Scouse Rogers took his ukulele back to the R.A.O.B. Club in Jarrow. They welcomed him there like a long-lost son. He sang and played to them and swung the lamp a bit, which was expected of him. He told them about Scapa and the wretched beer in the canteen there, which called for another pint on the spot. He tried to give them some idea of the splendours and miseries of destroyer life. The story of Paddy's codfish got a big laugh. One old Geordie said that it was the only fishing story he had ever heard where the big 'un didn't get away. They had a laugh together, too, over Rogers' description of old Tusky Hales, the Chief Gunner's Mate, and his pet theory about the ship. This took the form of a gloomy prophecy about the *Kelly*'s future.

'I tell you, lads,' old Tusky would say, 'the centre of gravity's too high in this ship. You mark my words. If a big sea hits her she'll turn right over; she'll go right over!'

'And she damn near did go over,' said Rogers, remembering that terrible moment and his oppo who was lost somewhere on the other side of the cold North Sea.

But all the world loves a singer, especially Irishmen and Geordies, and most of the time Rogers sang and played the uke. He gave them 'Roll Out the Barrel', which had become a hot favourite aboard ship, and they all joined in. They pestered him, too, for some of the naval songs he had picked up, and he gave them 'The Chief Stoker's Lament', a favourite among his messmates. He sang:

> Down in the stokehold there's all sorts of jobs,
> Priming and topping and sorting out cobs.
> Oh Chiefie, oh Chiefie, there's none here, I cried!
> Well, you'll jolly soon find some if I hop inside!

Hold your row, what d'yer say,
We'll rob all chief stokers who come down our way.

Then he would give them the chorus, singing:

She's a tiddley ship, on the ocean she'll skip,
She's sailing by night and by day,
And when she's in motion she's the pride of the
  ocean,
You can't see her sternpiece for spray.

Side, side, *Kelly*'s ship's side, Jimmy looks on it with
  pride.
He'd have a blue fit if he saw someone spit
On the side of the *Kelly*'s ship's side!

Of course there was no censor present when he sang it, so the real version was a little richer for a few blunt words here and there. But the chorus might have been written for the *Kelly* and Rogers could sing it with full relish. One little song he did not sing at the R.A.O.B. Club was the Navy's stock dripping song:

Roll on the *Rodney*, *Nelson*, *Renown*,
This one-funnelled bastard is getting me down.

They had sung that in Arctic waters, but here the Arctic was forgotten.

Rogers was speaking for all the Kellys when he told his people that life ashore on Tyneside was made happy for him by the good people of Jarrow and Hebburn. When he went ashore nothing was too good for him. The men of the shipyards and their wives proved to be the most generous and kind-hearted people in the world, in spite of the fact that they had, within recent memory, been through a period of black despair and suffering, when there was no work on Tyneside and desperation had driven the hunger-marchers from Jarrow to London. A weak personality is broken by such want and poverty as the Geordies had endured, but these strong people it only made stronger, wiser and deeper-marked with tolerance and kindness.

The men who had built the *Kelly* now turned to and patched her up. Between cleaning the salt water out of the boiler-feed water tanks and repairing the heavy-weather damage, it took them nearly a month to make her shipshape again, shipshape and, not Bristol, but one better than that – Hebburn fashion.

The matelots were glad of that month. They rested, feasted, went on leave and generally got some of the Arctic cold out of their bones. One or two of them started going steady with Tyneside girls and were soon taken to the bosom of the family – a happy state, known in the Navy as 'up homers'. Happy were the feet under the table and the hats on the hallstand.

They had only been in the Tyne a few days, when a shadow fell upon their homecoming jubilation. The news came through that the merchant-cruiser *Rawalpindi* had been sunk in action south of Iceland.

In darkness and heavy weather the German battle-cruisers *Scharnhorst* and *Gneisenau* had eluded our patrols when they came upon the merchant-cruiser. The *Rawalpindi* fought the heavy ships until every gun was silent and she floated, a blazing wreck, on the sea.

Later the Prime Minister spoke their epitaph:

'They must have known as soon as they sighted the enemy that there was no chance for them, but they had no thought of surrender. They fought their guns till they could be fought no more. They then – many of them – went to their deaths, and thereby carried on the great traditions of the Royal Navy. The example will be an inspiration to those who come after them.'

A matelot wouldn't say as much as that. But the spirit of it would fly from ship to ship, imperceptibly, like rumour. Men would remember old messmates lost, and recall distant runs ashore they had shared, so that the dead seemed not dead at all, only on draft to another ship, a ship on a distant foreign commission half-way across the world.

Another of the *Kelly*'s armed-merchant-cruiser friends, the ex-Aberdeen & Commonwealth liner *Jervis Bay*, was in the Tyne at the same time. Men from the two ships' companies used to meet ashore and yarn together over a pint. The *Kelly* men discovered that the *Jervis Bay* had a pet, a little black mongrel dog called George, whom, from all accounts, they did not treat too well. The destroyer had a pet already of course, the queenly Hawthorn, but they talked it over and decided to make the other ship an offer for George. The *Jervis Bay* was only too glad to get rid of George, and one of the *Kelly* men bought the little dog off them for a shilling.

He was a forlorn little dog when they brought him on board. The man who had bought him carried him down the ladder and set him down on the deck. George stood there for a moment, turning his head from side to side and looking at the unfamiliar surroundings with sad eyes. Then he looked up at his new messmates standing round him and gave a little whine.

'Poor little sod!' said one. 'He's as skinny as a bilge rat.'

'Yes, needs a good bath an' all,' said another, 'and a square meal under his waterline.'

'Well, a square meal he shall have. You'd like some big eats, wouldn't you, me old flower, eh?'

George was picked up and sat down on the lockers while the mess caterer got out some juicy scraps of meat that he had been saving for his oppo when he came off leave that night. But George only sniffed at the meat and gave another little whine.

'Blimey, what *are* we going to give him?' They all scratched their heads.

'Oh, give him some pusser's duff!' The mess caterer shook his head sadly and took down a saucer full of his own special brand of duff and custard.

'Lofty'll have to go hungry, that's all there is to it,' he

said, and set the somewhat solid mass down in front of the dog. George gave a yelp and dived into the saucer. First the custard was lapped up in about ten seconds flat, then the duff itself disappeared into the lean little belly. When he had licked up the last drop of custard and the last currant George looked at his oppos and barked and barked and barked. Then he trotted across the table and licked the hand that had fed him.

'Well, we'll have to keep you,' said the mess caterer; '*you* appreciate good cooking when you taste it.'

George never lost his appetite for pusser's duff, but they could never persuade him to eat meat. Another of the little dog's strongest characteristics was a marked preference for the lower deck. He was always for'ard with the lads, unlike Hawthorn, who was a proper Wren cat, forever down aft with the gold braid.

With a new whaler, motor-boat and guardrails, and a new pet aboard, the *Kelly* was about ready to leave Hebburn again, when they heard some heartening news from abroad. A German commerce-raider, which had been doing heavy damage in the South Atlantic and Indian Oceans, had been caught by a British squadron, and driven, badly battered, into the River Plate. Then came the report that she had scuttled herself off Montevideo. Between them, the *Exeter*, *Ajax* and *Achilles* had ended the career of a pocket battleship

Chalk it up on the scoreboard. Opposite *Rawalpindi* write *Graf Spee.*

That night they had the wireless on aboard when they heard the familiar voice of Lord Haw-Haw.

' . . . And where is your Lord Louis Mountbatten?' asked the jackass of Berlin Radio. 'You mustn't imagine we don't know. We do. He is on the Tyne *But he will never leave it.*'

'Custom cannot stale his infinite variety,' said someone in the wardroom

But it was something to think about, all the same. Next

day the *Kelly* and the destroyer *Mohawk* steamed down the Tyne, marked ships.

Haw-Haw's was not entirely an empty threat. He had behind him the *fait accompli* of the great damage already done to our shipping by Hitler's latest 'secret weapon', the magnetic mine. This new type of mine was not moored in the ordinary way and could not be swept by normal methods. It did not rely on contact with a ship to sink it, but was detonated by the ship's own magnetism. Almost from the beginning of the war German aircraft began dropping these mines in the harbours and river mouths round Great Britain, and the rate of sinkings by this method began to rise alarmingly. Once it could be produced in large numbers this new weapon could cripple British shipping, unless a counter-measure could be found. By December this counter-measure had been discovered. The answer to the magnetic mine was found to be the fitting of electric cables around the hulls of ships so as to reduce their magnetism, a process known as 'de-gaussing'. But the fitting of electric cables to all the ships using British ports was a job of such magnitude that it did not begin to get properly under way until 1940. Meanwhile the Germans continued to use the weapon that was to win the war.

Just before the evening when the *Kelly* and the *Mohawk* steamed slowly up the Tyne a number of mines had been laid in the river mouth. The destroyers received a signal:

> Two oil-tankers in trouble position 055 degrees 05 minutes north, 001 degrees 07 minutes west. U-boats believed in area. Proceed to area and intercept.

One or two men thought of Haw-Haw's warning when they heard about the signal. The *Kelly* picked up speed and went down river faster than was really safe in that treacherous stream. As she passed Jarrow Staithes a big merchantman nearly rammed her. The water boiled and foamed and she went full astern to avoid a collision. The Groyne fog bell sounded a mournful knell as the ship passed, and the doleful sound rang in the ears of the men on deck as the *Kelly* cleared the breakwater at Shields.

Once clear of the piers, the two destroyers went full speed ahead to the signalled position. When they arrived the ships were both sinking. One was well down by the stern, the other burning furiously and going down slowly. Both were victims of mines. The destroyers separated and proceeded to pick up survivors, the *Mohawk* going over to the more lightly damaged ship and the *Kelly* to the burning tanker.

Commander Evans was shaving in his cabin, when he felt a bump right under his feet. He passed it off as the other destroyer dropping depth-charges. Then there was a sudden, shattering crash, the razor slipped and he cut himself. It was a mine.

Down below on the messdecks they had been having tea. Then they all felt a series of heavy bumps.

'We're going alongside the tanker,' said someone. It was a case of 'famous last words'. The speaker was immediately flung violently into the air. There was a rush for the ladder, everyone getting in each other's way as the alarm bells rang in their ears.

Up on deck the loud bang shocked everyone's eardrums, and the plating shook underfoot. Astern, a mountain of white water hung in the air for a second, then fell with a crash on the stern of the ship. There was a rush to close all watertight doors and hatches.

The mine had bumped the ship three times without exploding and passed right between the propeller shafts, actually hitting one of the propellers, until it finally burst just clear of the stern. The explosion wrenched the stern several feet out of line and twisted the propellers. The *Kelly* lay, stopped and helpless in the water, a sitting target for any U-boat that might come upon her. The tiller flat, right aft, was partly flooded, and the after magazine bulkhead had to be shored up. Most of the water inside the ship, however, had got into the after compartment through the open hatches when the great volume of water flung up by the explosion had fallen on the stern section, and there was very little leakage.

A party of seamen worked down in the flooded tiller flat all night, while the ship was being towed back to the Tyne, getting ropes and wires and other gear out of the compartment and up on deck.

Perhaps the best comment on the whole episode was made in the wheelhouse by person unknown. A split second after the explosion an outraged voice exclaimed:

'Blimey, I bin done!'

Undoubtedly the man who had the severest shaking aboard was the seaman torpedo-man on watch right aft as depth-charge sentry. He was flung six feet into the air by the force of the bursting mine, landed again on his feet and ran a few yards for'ard before collapsing with shock. But he was soon in good shape again and was the first down the gangway when the *Kelly* docked once more in Hebburn.

To say that the dockyard mateys were surprised to see them would be putting it very mildly indeed. They were flabbergasted.

'But you only went out yesterday afternoon,' said one Geordie in blank amazement.

'Couldn't stand being parted from you, mate,' said Nobby Clarke.

Those who drew their tots saw a very melancholy sight when the water was drained from the drydock. The ship's rum store had been broken open by the explosion and rich, black, Jamaica rum could now be seen dripping slowly on to the bottom of the dock. A little group gathered on the side of the dock, staring miserably at the leak.

'You can smell it,' said one man, 'from 'ere.'

'Yes,' said another grog man. 'It's like watching your own life blood flowing away, drop by drop.'

Christmas was only a few days away when they docked, but all of them were broke and had few hopes of getting home for the festive season.

However, they got their leave after all. Lady Mountbatten, who had always kept a close eye on the welfare of her husband's ship, paid every man's fare home. Before they left the ship on fourteen days' leave Captain Mountbatten cleared lower deck and wished them all a happy Christmas, telling them that they were undoubtedly the luckiest ship's company in the navy to get *two* lots of Christmas leave.

Captain Mountbatten and some of his staff went by train to Portland, where Mountbatten commanded the rest of the Fifth Flotilla from the *Kelvin.* In fact they did not rejoin the *Kelly* until the end of February, when she was ready for sea again.

So they went off happily on leave, all except one.

When the mine had bumped amidships, a young stoker, already unnerved by the fearful thought that the ship might be hit and sink, trapping him below, had suddenly left his post and rushed up the ladder from the boiler-room in a wild panic.

Desertion of duty in the face of the enemy poses a difficult problem of discipline and morale to any commanding officer. Mountbatten met it in a singular way.

When the wretched young man was brought before him he could tell that fear and shame had already created their own punishment.

'Do you know the penalty for deserting your post in the face of the enemy?' he asked.

'Yes, sir,' whispered the miserable man, 'death.'

'Good,' said Mountbatten. 'I shall stand this case over and deal with it later.'

The man was led away, white-faced and trembling violently. Two hours later Mountbatten cleared lower deck and spoke to the ship's company.

'Today,' he said, 'we have been through one of the

most trying experiences which can befall a newly commissioned ship in war. We have had to endure the suspense of feeling a mine bumping along the bottom, waiting every moment for it to explode. Fortunately it was not a very good mine, and did not go off until it reached the propellers. Out of two hundred and forty men on board this ship, two hundred and thirty-nine behaved as they ought to have, and as I expected them to behave, but one was unable to control himself and deserted his post, and incidentally his comrades, in the engine-room. I had him brought before me a couple of hours ago, and he himself informed me that he knew the punishment for desertion of his post could be death. You will therefore be surprised to know that I propose to let him off with a caution, one caution to him and a second one to myself, for having failed in four months to impress my personality and doctrine on each and all of you to prevent such an incident from occurring. From now on I will try to make it clear that I expect everyone to behave in the way the two hundred and thirty-nine did, and to stick to their post in action to the last. I will under no circumstances whatever again tolerate the slightest suspicion of cowardice or indiscipline, and I know from now on that none of you will present me with any such problem.'

When the *Kelly* left the Tyne again she went back to Scapa and was soon on the same weary run of patrols and escort work.

Life aboard was grim, although the stokers were lucky in having a George Formby on the messdeck. Rogers did not exactly sing for his supper, but if he were to pick up the dish rag after supper and start wiping up, one of his messmates would be sure to say:

'Don't do that, Rog. Give it to me and you go and give us a tune on the old uke.'

So he would play and sing for them and they would join in. The music would drift up through the hatch to the seamen's messdeck, and the men there would start up a counter-melody. So music relieved the weary round, music and the unfailing ability of the matelot to squeeze a laugh from the bitterest fruit.

One afternoon, after dinner, Rogers took the dirty washing-up water on deck and ditched it down the gash-chute into the sea. There happened to be one or two forgotten eating irons left in the bottom of the mess kettle. These rattled out now and disappeared overboard.

'Tinkle, tinkle, little spoon, knife and fork will follow soon,' said a voice from the flagdeck above.

Gordon came down the ladder into the mess with a worried look on his face.

'Hey, Hookie,' he said to the leading hand of the mess, 'is a thing lost if you know where it is?'

'Of course it isn't, you silly sod,' said the leading hand.

'Then all the knives, forks and spoons aren't lost. I *know* they're on the bottom of the sea,' said Gordon.

For some time Captain Mountbatten had been trying to work out some method of indicating a sudden attack by mine or torpedo. The destroyer *Exmouth* had recently disappeared with all hands, without trace and without making a single signal to describe her fate or show her position. One day at sea Lieutenant Dunsterville called Chief Petty Officer Primrose to his cabin.

'Chief, have you heard about the *Exmouth*?' he asked.

'Yes, sir,' said Primrose. 'Sunk with all hands, wasn't she?'

'Yes, with no signals to say what had happened to her. Well, we don't want that to happen to us. I want you to put this procedure into operation at once. If the petty officer on watch hears an explosion and it seems to him we've been hit he will immediately make the signal, "Have been hit by mine or torpedo. Am uncertain which." Clear?'

'Yes, sir, quite clear,' said Primrose.

A short time after this they were escorting a convoy in northern waters. It had been very dirty weather for days on end, and a heavy snowstorm had reduced visibility almost to zero. Things were so bad that Leading Seaman Jimmy Grub was moved to ask:

'Is everything all right aft?'

'Yes, why?' said someone.

'Oh, nothing,' said Jimmy. 'It's just that I haven't been able to see abaft the funnel for two days. I thought the after part was steaming on its own.'

He had hardly got these words out when there was a terrible jarring crash. Those on deck saw a dark shape sweep past them in the blinding snow, then vanish astern.

Primrose had had his head down in the mess. He was awakened instantly by the crash and rushed outside just in time to hear 'Hands to collision stations' being piped. He went straight to the wireless office, fearing the worst. It was too late. He heard the signal going out as he came through the door.

'Have been hit by mine or torpedo. Am uncertain which.' Primrose swore.

'How many times have you sent that?' he asked.

'Only once, Chief,' said the petty officer.

'Thank God for that,' said Primrose. 'Make the erase at the double – it's a collision. We'll be the laughing stock of the Fleet.'

But once had been enough. As Primrose put the high frequency phones to his ears, he was just in time to catch the ribald signal:

'*Kelly* from *Gurkha*. That was me, not mine.'

The destroyer *Gurkha* had been escorting a southbound convoy steaming in the opposite direction. Although the two convoys were routed well clear of each other, in the appalling weather the southbound convoy had had difficulty in fixing its position with the result that the flank destroyers of the two convoys had overlapped.

Destroyer captains dined out on this incident for many months. Nevertheless, the signal was later adopted as official procedure.

The two ships had seen each other just in time to avoid a really dangerous collision. But, in turning away, the *Gurkha*'s propeller-guard had torn a long gash in the *Kelly*'s bow.

The Chief Shipwright had just come out of the mess after the crash, when he bumped into Lieutenant Robin.

'Come with me, Chippy,' said Guns. They started searching for'ard for the damage. As they got to the boys' messdeck, they began to feel a strong sea breeze. Going into the messdeck, they saw a great split in the ship's side about thirty feet long. Not two feet away from the gash one of the boys was sleeping peacefully in his hammock.

They were forced to leave the convoy while they lay to and lashed torpedo mats over the hole, hoping that the snowstorm would screen them, both from U-boats and from the bombers that were attacking the convoy at the time.

Eventually they limped back to home waters and put into Lerwick, in the Shetlands. There they worked all night making temporary repairs, covering the hole with mess tables and forms. At five a.m. Chippy was able to report, 'Ship's side temporarily repaired.' The Captain immediately ordered the engine-room to raise steam for twenty-six knots, to test the repairs. With this makeshift stopper in the hole they were able to make Scapa, where a further temporary repair job was done by the depot ship, plates being welded over the split.

All northern drydocks were full at that time, so the *Kelly* was forced to return to southern waters for her major repairs. When she eventually berthed in the London Graving Dock everyone anticipated leave. They felt that they had deserved it.

CHAPTER VI

'KEEP ON'

THE *Kelly* docked in London on the third day of March. It was a homecoming. Most of the men were from Chatham depot and lived within easy striking distance of their lucky landfall. The others went swiftly up the line to their homes.

The men left aboard kicked their heels, waiting their turn for leave, watching the repair work going on and singing:

> See the dockyard mateys' children, sitting on the dockyard wall,
> Just like their fathers, doing damn all.
> When they grow older they'll be dockyard mateys too,
> Just like their fathers, damn all to do.

During the few weeks they were in dock the Kellys had several distinguished guests. Royalty visited the ship on more than one occasion. The King and Queen paid their cousin a visit and dined quietly on board, and the two young Princesses came several times to the London Graving Dock, accompanied by their dogs.

The *Kelly*'s own dog, now a good deal fatter for several months of good pusser's duff, very nearly went adrift. One leading seaman had grown particularly attached to the little mongrel, and one day, when the *Kelly* was at Sheerness towards the end of her sojourn down south, he took the opportunity to give his messmate a treat and took him 'up homers' with the family at Woolwich. When he rejoined the ship George stayed behind at home.

Soon it was all round the ship that the mascot was missing. When he heard the news, Captain Mountbatten sent for the leading hand.

'Well, where is our mascot?' asked Mountbatten.

'I don't know, sir. I think he must have done a dockside jump in London and got lost.'

'I see. Well, here is your fare home. Now I suggest that *you* go ashore and get lost until you find him. That is all.'

The next day George was back eating duff and custard on the messdeck.

So the weeks went by. To the *Kelly* men this was all highday and holiday after Scapa. But while they were in dock events outside were boiling up for the big explosion. The twilight war was growing darker and its shadow was lengthening over a peaceful country.

From the very beginning of the war the ostrich of Norwegian neutrality had had her head deep in the sand. That was the only way she could negotiate a compromising situation, an undignified if not quite a dishonourable way, in the face of grim facts such as the daily murder of Norwegian seamen on the high seas by German U-boats, and the flagrant abuse of Norwegian territorial waters by German ships. The *City of Flint* had been one notable case of this strange reading of the term 'neutrality', but on

February 16th something happened which very nearly touched off a highly volatile situation.

Three hundred British merchant seamen, taken off prizes sunk by the *Graf Spee*, had been transferred to the German 'prison ship' *Altmark*. The *Altmark* was now in Jossingfiord, south of Stavanger, sheltering in Norwegian territorial waters. Captain Vian, in the destroyer *Cossack*, was ordered to board the *Altmark* and rescue her prisoners. This was done, and the Norwegian Government immediately complained loudly of the violation of her territorial waters by a British ship. The British Government replied by underlining the almost habitual use of these waters by German ships, and were so convinced by this latest episode of the absolute advantage given to Germany by the present Norwegian attitude that they very nearly took the besmirched law into their own hands.

There were many reasons why Norway was of such vital importance to us. Our main concern was to stop the flow of iron ore from Narvik in northern Norway down through the Inner Leads to Germany. The *Altmark* incident nearly gave the British Government the justification it needed to mine the Leads, so driving German shipping out into the open.

But the mining operation was postponed at the last minute, and a larger plan, which had been in preparation for some time, was again considered. By this plan the Allies were to occupy certain strategic parts of Norway to prevent a German occupation. Besides uninterrupted access to the Swedish iron ore, possession of Norway would give Germany bases practically on Britain's doorstep from which a much heavier attack on British defences, industry and shipping could be mounted, and from which she could give greater protection to her own shipping. This serious threat to the Allies had been increased greatly by the Russian attack on Finland on November 30th, and the plan was given as its main goal the rescue of Finland. The main force was to land at

Narvik in mid-March and advance through the Swedish orefield to the port of Lulea. A second force would take three strategic ports in southern Norway, Trondheim, and its satellite Namos, Bergen, and Stavanger, where the airfield, the nearest to Scapa Flow, would be destroyed. In addition, the plan provided for a campaign in southern Sweden. If the plan were put into operation the Home Fleet would have its hands full. One hundred thousand men would have to be convoyed across the North Sea, for which at least forty destroyers would be needed as escorts.

But it was not put into operation. The Finnish surrender on March 13th put an end to it. The Scandinavian Governments now withdrew whatever timid sympathy they had given to the scheme and the British Government did not want to risk pushing them into the enemy camp.

Instead, the former idea of mining the Leads was revived. It was taken for granted that Germany would react immediately to such a step by moving against Norway, and plans were made to defend the country by occupying Narvik and the three southern ports, as in the previous plan.

On the early morning of April 8th eight British destroyers, under the protection of the battle-cruiser *Renown* and eight Allied destroyers, began laying a minefield in the approaches to the Vestfiord, north of Bodo. Two more destroyers laid the second field off Bud, near Molde.

Then, suddenly, the northern minelaying force was ordered to abandon its work and rejoin the *Renown*. The German Fleet was at sea.

Almost step by step with the British, German plans had been going forward for the taking of Norway. Hitler, in his turn, wanted to beat Britain to the punch. The *Altmark* rescue finally showed him which way the wind blew, and a close study of the possibilities of an attack on Norway and Denmark was begun. The German plan was, of necessity, based on the idea of a bloodless occupation –

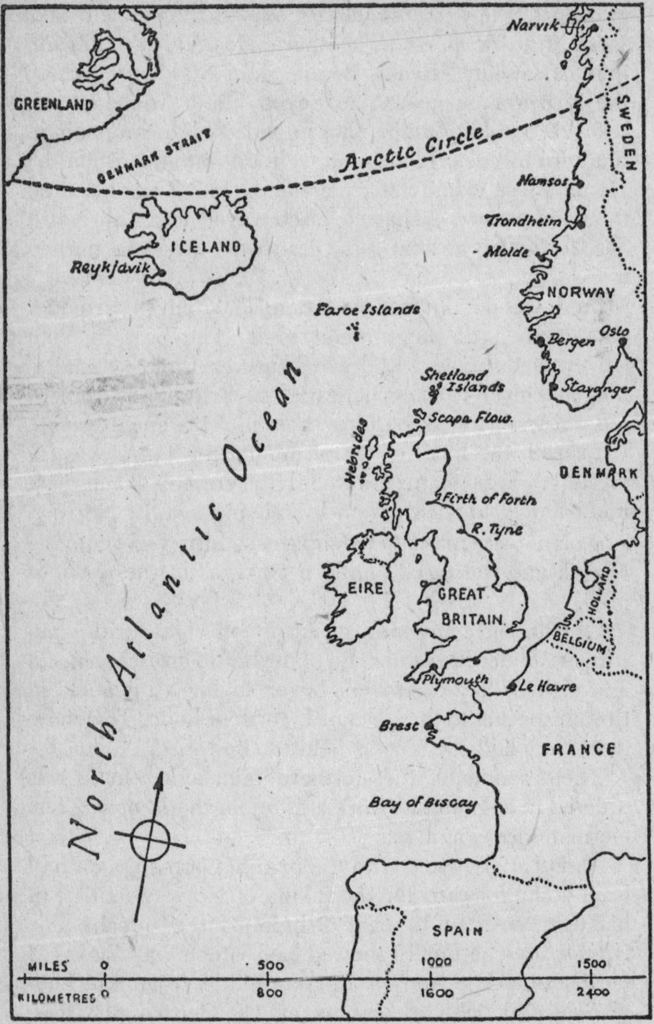
GREENLAND
DENMARK STRAIT
Arctic Circle
ICELAND
Reykjavik
Narvik
SWEDEN
Namsos
Trondheim
Molde
NORWAY
Faroe Islands
Bergen
Oslo
Shetland Islands
Stavanger
Scapa Flow
North Atlantic Ocean
Hebrides
DENMARK
Firth of Forth
R. Tyne
EIRE
GREAT BRITAIN
HOLLAND
BELGIUM
Plymouth
Le Havre
Brest
FRANCE
Bay of Biscay
SPAIN
MILES 0 500 1000 1500
KILOMETRES 0 800 1600 2400

by speed and secrecy from without, and treachery from within. The Nazis could count on one great advantage over the Allies. They did not have to wait upon Norwegian and Danish goodwill, only upon the success of their Fifth Column in Norway and the cover of bad weather and darkness for the coup.

So the two plans rushed forward neck and neck. But the Germans got their blow in first. On April 9th they delivered their ultimatum to Norway and Denmark. Denmark immediately submitted to occupation, but Norway resisted, crippled though she was by the Quisling element. German forces crossed the Skagerak and captured Oslo. The German Navy carried troops to capture Kristiansand, Bergen, Trondheim and Narvik, and Stavanger was occupied. The Luftwaffe quickly moved in and soon had a force of four hundred bombers in the air. British forces counter-attacked and two brilliant destroyer actions cleared Narvik of the enemy. But the Germans were advancing on Trondheim, and central Norway was almost in their hands. A small Allied force was landed on either side of Trondheim, one at Namsos, to the north-east, and one at Aandalsnes, to the south-west. These two forces were to converge upon Trondheim.

When Major-General Carton de Wiart, V.C., and the men of Mauriceforce landed at Namsos they found a beautiful little town and harbour, fifteen miles up from the end of the lovely Nansenfiord. It was a town of little painted wooden houses, with a stone railway quay, two wooden wharves and a good anchorage for ships.

The army had been preceded in Namsos by a naval force, which had been landed by destroyers on April 14th. They were under continuous air observation by the enemy, and when General de Wiart arrived by flying-boat on the 15th he flew straight into a heavy air raid. On that day the first contingent of Mauriceforce arrived. They had been transferred to destroyers in a remote channel farther north so as to dodge the Luftwaffe. By the evening of the

17th they were ashore, though the area was bombed continuously. They advanced rapidly through the heavy snow towards Steinkjer, on the road to Trondheim. As they moved forward the French contingent of Chasseurs Alpins moved into Namsos. Their convoy had been under heavy air attack all the way up the fiord, and they were hurried ashore as fast as possible.

There was no landing ground in the area and no aircraft-carriers were available, so de Wiart's men had no protection from the air. Namsos was bombed without respite right throughout the 20th. The bright little wooden houses, the railway, the wooden wharves and most of the stone quay were burned or blown to pieces and the French headquarters were hit. That night the destroyer *Nubian* steamed up the fiord and saw Namsos burning, a sea of fire, at the other end of the darkness. By then the doom of Mauriceforce was in the air. General de Wiart reported, 'I see little chance of carrying out decisive or, indeed, any operations, unless enemy air activity is considerably restricted.'

But the bombing continued, for there was nothing to stop it. British destroyers continued to give him what help they could against the bombers. But they could not stave off the inevitable. Bombed and blasted, Mauriceforce had shot its bolt. On the 28th General de Wiart received orders to evacuate his force, in conjunction with a general withdrawal from central Norway. His troops were to be taken off in two batches, one on the night of May 1st/2nd, the other on the following night.

On April 29th a force of warships and transports had sailed from Scapa Flow for Namsos. They were bombed on May 1st on their way across the North Sea, and in the evening they ran into thick fog forty miles short of their rendezvous, the Kya Light, and eighty miles short of Namsos. This made the evacuation schedule for that night out of the question and it was cancelled. However, as the tired men lined up on Namsos quayside dispersed and scattered to wait for the following night, they saw the sharp bows of a destroyer break through the mist into the clear light above the town.

It was the *Kelly*. All through those last weeks of April as she lay in dock, reports were coming in of fierce and bloody naval engagements being fought in Norwegian waters. They heard of the *Renown*'s battle in a snowstorm with the *Scharnhorst* and *Gneisenau*. Mountbatten heard with mixed feelings of sadness and pride of the splendid fight of his friend Warburton-Lee and his destroyers in the first battle for Narvik, which cost Captain Warburton-Lee his life. These two officers had been friendly rivals in pre-war days in the Mediterranean, when Mountbatten had commanded the destroyer *Wishart* and Warburton-Lee the *Witch*. Then followed the news of the glorious Second Battle of Narvik, when the entire enemy force of destroyers that had brought the German force to Narvik was destroyed.

The *Kelly*'s repairs were speeded up. Every destroyer would be needed in support of the army in Norway. When, eventually, it was clearly seen that the end was near, that need became vital, almost desperate.

The *Kelly* entered Scapa on April 29th. Immediately Mountbatten was summoned to a commanding officers' conference, where arrangements were discussed for the disembarkation of the Namsos force. Mountbatten was given a mixed flotilla of four British destroyers and one French. He wondered grimly how many of these he would lead back across the North Sea after two successive nights spent in the narrow waters of a fiord under a sky alive with dive-bombers.

The air raid in the North Sea gave them their first taste of what lay ahead. Then came the fog, thick and widespread. It stopped the rescuing force in its tracks and they stumbled in circles round the Kya Light.

But the fog gave Captain Mountbatten an idea. If fog could hide Namsos from them, it might also hide the

British ships from German bombers. He asked permission to take his flotilla and make a dash for Namsos. Permission was given, and the *Kelly* led the other four ships along the coast towards Nansenfiord.

It was seventy miles of fog, seventy miles of rocky, treacherous coastline. Once the *Kelly* escaped running into a jagged ridge of rock, when the fog cleared just two hundred yards ahead of her bows. But they hugged the fog and were thankful for it, thinking of the bombers.

So they dodged from fogbank to fogbank, with the hungry planes moaning overhead. At last they found the entrance of the fiord and started their suicide dash up the narrow waterway to the beleaguered town.

All the way they were bombed. No direct hits were scored, but a near miss on one of the ships killed or injured twenty-three men. Although from the decks of the ships they could see nothing of the enemy, all unbeknown to them their masts were sticking out above the fog. The Germans tied themselves to the trucks of the masts and unloaded their bombs.

Another thing they did not know was that the sky above Namsos itself was free of fog. When they shot out of the fog and saw the burning town in clear light before them, the bombers fastened on them like wolves. It was impossible to evacuate any men under such conditions. They turned into the fog again and steamed back down the fiord to the sea.

The next day dawned, the last day for the evacuation. Still the whole naval force lay fogbound. In the evening the situation was getting desperate, when the ships suddenly ran out into clear visibility, about forty miles from Nansenfiord. Immediately Admiral Cunningham divided his force into two groups. He himself, with two cruisers and four destroyers, stayed in position near the Kya Light while the cruiser *York* with five destroyers and the three transports went to Namsos.

By this time the advancing German forces had almost

caught up with the British rearguard holding out on the hills behind Namsos. It was going to be touch and go.

The *Kelly* led the van at twenty-six knots. The sun had gone down by now, but twilight gleamed softly on the hills and quiet valleys on either hand. Smoke curled up gently from farmhouses. Quietness and peace lay everywhere.

Then they turned the last bend and came upon burning, battered Namsos. It was their first sight of the results of blitzkrieg from the air.

At that point no one knew whether the town was still in our hands or whether the Germans were now in occupation. If they were, they would almost certainly have guns bearing on the harbour. Just ahead of the *Kelly* a wrecked anti-submarine trawler, the *Aston Villa,* lay burning, and several other small craft lay wrecked around the harbour.

They looked at the town itself. Everything was ablaze – houses, church, jetties and great piles of stores on the quay. Against this background of fire six thousand troops were lined up, waiting to be taken off.

Two of the transports went straight alongside the quay and started to fill up with troops. The destroyers took off the other men and ferried them in batches out to the *York* and the third transport, before taking a final load themselves. The operation began at half-past ten that night, and by twenty minutes past two the following morning the last batch of troops had been taken off by the destroyer *Afridi.* The *Kelly*'s particular guests were all Chasseurs Alpins. The *Kelly* men gave them cigarettes and made them as comfortable as possible. The French troops all carried very heavy packs, many of them made heavier by the weight of whole cheeses which the Frenchmen refused to leave behind for German barbarians to stuff down their brutish gullets.

The *Afridi* was the last ship to leave and strike out for the open sea. There had been no time for any systematic 'spiking the guns', so, as the destroyer pulled away from the jetty, her guns shelled the groups of vehicles and dumps of equipment left behind there. Then she went full speed down the fiord.

They knew they were in for it when daylight broke. They were far beyond the range of fighter escort and could look forward to an uncomfortable return journey.

At half-past four the rear section of the retreating fleet was sighted by the enemy and it was only a short time before the Luftwaffe appeared. The force was attacked continuously until late afternoon. The two transports, one cruiser and escorting destroyers were drawn up in a defensive formation of single line ahead, with the anti-aircraft cruiser *Carlisle* last in the line. In the third attack of the day the French destroyer of Mountbatten's group, the *Bison,* was badly hit and set on fire. The other destroyers immediately turned back to pick up survivors, whom the Germans were machine-gunning in the water. It was while she was engaged in this errand of mercy that the *Afridi* was hit by two heavy bombs. She capsized with the loss of one hundred men.

The damage had been done by dive-bombers, hurtling down at a steep angle and from a great height. This was the first time the *Kelly* had been attacked by these screaming monsters. The warships knocked down several of their attackers, and the *Kelly*'s pom-pom scored its first kill.

Eventually they regained the shelter of Scapa Flow. Here they remained for two days. When they had all got their second wind, the *Kelly* saw her charges safely home to the Clyde. Hardly had she dropped anchor off Greenock, before she was ordered to refuel at once and proceed to the East Coast.

On the way round the ship's company were told that the *Kelly* was to join up with the cruiser *Birmingham* and a destroyer force and endeavour to bring to action a German force composed of a minelayer and E-boats which had been located near the Island of Sylt. They steamed round the Scottish coast and entered the Firth of Forth, but, once again, no sooner had they put their nose in than they were ordered out again to a rendezvous farther south.

On joining the main force in the afternoon they found another of their own flotilla, the *Kandahar,* among them,

About six o'clock in the evening the *Kandahar* reported that she had contacted a submarine. She and the *Kelly* were at once ordered to hunt the contact. Depth-charge attacks proved unsuccessful, and, with dusk approaching, Captain Mountbatten decided to rejoin the main force.

Another flotilla was operating to the north-east of the *Kelly,* and after sunset gun-flashes were seen in that direction. Meanwhile, the destroyer *Bulldog,* which did not belong to the *Kelly*'s flotilla, had lost contact with her own flotilla and signalled to the *Kelly* asking for permission to join her. The signal was approved, but the *Bulldog* was a long way astern. She followed up at high speed.

In the failing light the two destroyers steamed on, with the *Bulldog* coming up on them.

Down in the *Kelly*'s engine-room the fuel situation was giving cause for anxiety. As long ago as noon the *Kelly* had made a signal giving the fuel state as forty-four per cent. Since then she and the *Kandahar* had been steaming at high speed and the fuel had been running steadily lower and lower in the tanks. Commander Evans was down in the engine-room working out the consumption every few minutes, estimating how much they would need to get back to port. As a result of what he told the Captain it was announced that they would proceed on their present course until eleven o'clock. If they had not rejoined the main force by that time they would be forced to break off and return to base. In the meantime they were told that they could fall out from action stations but must remain ready to fall in again at a moment's notice.

Bob Knight and Bert Male shared the same action station, in the cross passageway on the main deck, amidships. As the sick bay was only one deck above, they went up there and sat reading for a while. Male's main dressing station in action was the wardroom, and he had prepared it hours before, getting out dressings, covering the table, fixing up the steriliser and switching it on to 'slow'. As they sat in the sick bay reading, Male glanced at his watch from time to time, and just before eleven o'clock he said:

'Bogey, I think I'll just slip along to the wardroom and switch off the steriliser and see if I can get the latest buzz.'

So Male left and made his way aft, leaving the writer sitting in the sick bay, between the cot and the bulkhead.

When Rogers was relieved off the second dog at eight o'clock in the for'ard boiler-room, he remained there at his action station, for at that time they kept a double watch below in case of injury. When the order to stand down temporarily from action stations came through the Chief Stoker said:

'Rogers, go to the 4.7s on the fo'c'sle and give them a hand with the ammunition supply.'

'O.K., Chief,' he replied. 'But what about my mate?'

'You'd better take him with you – they're short-handed up there,' said the Chief.

Gordon motioned to his oppo and they went up the ladder. Once out of the noise of the forced-draught fans of the boiler-room he told the younger man what they had to do. Rogers was no green hand now, but a fully-fledged first-class stoker and, so he thought, a real old campaigner.

'Come on,' he said to the second-class stoker, 'we'd better go to the messdeck and put on some warm gear if we're going up on the fo'c'sle.'

When they reached the guns they were given their orders and settled down to wait the watch through. One of the gun's crew took pity on Rogers, who, in spite of his extra clothing, was feeling the change from the heat of the boiler-room to the cold night air.

'Hey, Stokes, come and park your arse on this valve.'

he said. Rogers was grateful for the shelter of the gun-shield and went to sit down on the valve.

In the chief petty officers' mess they were taking it easy. 'Chippy', still on light duties after a bad hernia contracted at Lerwick when he was repairing the ship's side after the collision with the *Gurkha,* was shivering on the upper deck, when the First Lieutenant said to him:

'Chippy, I should go and get a hot drink inside you; we shan't be catching up with them for another hour.'

So he went to the mess and found that the messmen had just made a cup of cocoa. He and Primrose and the Chief Ordnance Artificer, and one or two others, sat around drinking their ky and chatting. Somehow the talk got round to conundrums and puzzles. Some of them drifted off to their stations, but four men stayed behind to tackle a puzzle that Chippy said he had never been able to solve. Primrose did not go down to the wireless office immediately. He had found a good Western and was sitting at the table reading it.

All the seamen off watch were sitting in their messes listening to the latest buzzes from the fire and repair parties, when they heard that the ship would be turning back in about five minutes.

Those on deck froze and blew on their hands, cursing all Jerry minelayers.

'Roll on my twelve,' said Nobby Clarke, up on 'B' gun, 'then I shall be happy. I can't see any minelayers. All I can see is mist and everlasting 'ogwash.'

Then suddenly he saw something else – a little white line of luminous foam away to port, heading straight for the ship.

Someone yelled:

'Torpedo!'

There was a terrible pause.

'Thank God that was a dud,' said the Captain.

Then the explosion came. The torpedo smashed into the

Kelly's plates right on the for'ard boiler-room and burst with a terrifying detonation.

A great lick of flame roared up into the night, the masthead silhouetted black and stark against its glare. Commander Evans saw it from the signal distributing office, where he had gone for information about the ship's movements. Some only heard the terrible blast that came with it. Some felt the great shock.

Some, including all those in the for'ard boiler-room, heard, saw and felt nothing. Nor would they ever again.

All around the heart of the wound men lay dead, dying, wounded and stunned. All were dazed by the shock. The ship lay over to starboard in a cloud of desperate, hissing steam and smoke, with a great hole torn in her side from her keel almost to her upper deck, all power gone, and, it seemed, all aboard her silent for ever.

Then nerves awoke and the numbness wore off. Hoarse orders, startled cries, mingled with the slow awakening of pain as the shocked and wounded found their small, thin voices. Voices first, then movement.

Commander Evans rushed to the bridge and told the Captain he was going below to assess the damage. He managed to claw his way into the flooded boiler-room, and reported back to the bridge that the for'ard boiler had been hurled aft and to starboard. This boiler had been developing twenty thousand horse-power when its boiling veins were torn open, releasing this shattering force inside the ship. Both boiler-rooms, he reported, and the after messdeck were full of water, but the bulkheads on either side of the flooded area seemed fairly sound. There was no power of course, and only emergency lighting.

Having made his report, the Commander returned below to see what could be done towards shoring up the damaged and bent bulkheads, and to prevent the flooding from spreading.

Luckily, the Fifth Flotilla was one of the first units in the Navy to have special damage control orders and a complete organisation to deal with damage. The damage and action repair parties went to work at once. The first thing to do was to get rid of all movable topweight, to stop the ship from capsizing. She was listing very badly to starboard, and the starboard gunwhale was awash. Depth charges were set to 'safe' and thrown overboard and all the ready-use ammunition ditched. All torpedoes were fired 'set to sink' and all the boats were lowered and cast off except the whaler, which was towed.

Rogers was thrown up against the roof of the gun-shield by the explosion. Luckily he was wearing his tin hat, and this undoubtedly saved him from a cracked skull. But if he had remained on watch below he would not have been alive now. He heard the Captain shout through a megaphone:

'Don't jump over the side until I give the order. The ship is not sinking, so don't panic.'

The explosion made itself felt up in the chiefs' mess, too. The deck there was torn across in a great gash and the place filled with bitter, acrid smoke. Primrose threw down his Western and made his way to the wireless office.

When he got there he realised that he owed his life to the book. If he had gone to his station in the office he would now be among the mangled dead and dying who lay buried in its shattered ruin. The entrance was blocked and one corner of the office was split open, like the corner of a cardboard box. A small party of men gathered there, determined to get through to the men inside.

First the Medical Officer tried to get through the crack, but it was far too narrow. Rogers arrived on the scene at this point.

'Give us that bar, Stokes,' said one man, 'there, under that bloke's head.'

Gently Rogers lifted the dead man's head and handed up the broken stanchion, aware of the tears pouring down his face. Between them they widened the crack. It was still too narrow, but a young telegraphist named O'Neill said:

'I'm only skinny – shove me through.'

They held the crack open, the doctor gave him a hypodermic full of morphia, and they pushed him through into the shambles beyond. Then the crack closed upon him. He must have known that if the ship sank at that moment there was no hope for him.

Meanwhile Bert Male was treating casualties down aft as fast as they came in. The wardroom was flooded so he could not use the carefully prepared dressings there. He had to make do with the first-aid tins he had placed in gun positions and other places all over the ship. Nearly all his patients were burned in some degree, besides suffering from many other injuries. He dressed their wounds and gave a shot of morphia wherever he thought necessary, then got them settled down while the Maltese steward prepared hot drinks for them all. It was then that he thought of Knight, whom he had left all alone in the sick bay, right over the for'ard boiler-room.

Bob came aft shortly and told his story. A great hole was torn in the deck of the sick bay right by his side. Only by instinctively grabbing the door curtains had he managed to stop himself from falling into the blazing hell below him. After what seemed like ages he dragged himself up the wrecked ladder to the signal-deck. By then his hands and face had been severely burned and the skin was hanging off in shreds. He remembered very little after that. But one thing remained permanently in his mind. In the midst of his great pain, Captain Mountbatten came up to him, took off his greatcoat and wrapped it round the petty officer.

So the injured were cared for and the ship made as seaworthy as a half-waterlogged vessel could be. No one had thought of abandoning ship. Most of the boats had been lowered and cast off immediately after the explosion, and both Carley floats had vanished, one having been sucked into the gaping hole left by the torpedo.

When the *Kandahar* saw the terrible flash of the torpedo striking the flotilla leader, and her men had searched vainly in the great pall of smoke and steam for signs of the other ship, they decided that she must have gone down. The young Marquess of Milford Haven, then on the eve of his twenty-first birthday, was Officer of the Watch at that time aboard the *Kandahar*, and his feelings when he saw, as he thought, his uncle's ship blown up and sunk before his eyes can be imagined.

The faithful *Bulldog* had by then come upon the scene, in time to send two hurried signals, first:

> From: BULLDOG
> To: ADMIRALTY.
> Kelly has been torpedoed 56.48 N. 05.09 E.

Then:

> To: SCAPA. BIRMINGHAM.
> Assistance required immediately my position 56.48 N. 05.33 E.

Meanwhile she came alongside the *Kelly* with a cool 'Where do you want us, sir?' After several unsuccessful attempts in that jet-black night, and with a high sea running and both ships pitching heavily, she managed to get a tow-line aboard the crippled ship and began to pull her slowly and painfully towards home.

Aboard the *Kelly* men were spread out in a human chain stretching from the bridge to the hatch leading to the tiller flat. Their job was to repeat all orders given by the Officer of the Watch to the ratings down in the tiller flat who were steering the ship by hand.

The only helm orders given throughout the tricky and tedious operation were 'Port thirty-five' or Starboard thirty-five' and 'Midships'. This got very monotonous as the long hours of darkness wore on. Down in the tiller flat they hardly had time to heave the wheel over, when the order came to reverse the rudder. But they changed round as often as possible and most people had a shot at one job or another during the night.

Just after midnight, when Captain Mountbatten was alone on the bridge, he heard the roaring sound of a high-speed petrol engine, and out of the inky blackness an E-boat appeared. She hit the *Bulldog* a glancing blow on the starboard quarter, bounced off and came scraping down the *Kelly*'s side at forty knots.

Primrose had just come out on deck. He was just in time to see the E-boat and its yelling, screaming crew, ride right up on to the canted deck in front of him and smash its way aft. The davits and guardrails which were dangling in the water tore the bottom out of the light craft and left planking and belts of twenty-millimetre ammunition on the deck of the *Kelly*. The boat disappeared in the darkness astern with her engines still running. Loud German screams tailed away into silence as she sank.

Leading Seaman Frankie Waite's oppo, 'Frankie' Fitt, had had a narrow escape. The ship's whaler had been lowered earlier with some idea of towing it astern. Fitt climbed down into it. Then Waite suddenly had a premonition.

'Frankie,' he shouted, 'grab this heaving line and come inboard again.' Fitt did so, and two minutes later the E-boat smashed into the whaler and swept boat and davits away.

Once again darkness and silence fell on the stricken ship. During the night the tow parted several times, and when the dawn came she was found to have increased her list and to be lower in the water.

At seven o'clock the ship's company spliced the mainbrace. The neat rum was very welcome after the long night of hard work and suspense. Then they braced themselves to face the day ahead. They were aboard a ship held together by a few steel girders and plates, a ship on the point of sinking, a ship that should have sunk already by all standards – by all standards save the *Kelly*'s.

With the daylight the *Kandahar* put her fo'c'sle alongside that of the *Kelly* and took off the wounded. The wounded gone, now came the task that everyone dreaded.

The Gunner (T), Mr Brownjohn, came up to Nobby Clarke and said:

'Petty Officer Clarke, the Captain would like you to find as many bodies as you can amongst the wreckage for'ard and sew them up in hammocks. We must give them a Christian burial.'

Nobby turned to his oppo.

'Come on, let's get cracking,' he said.

When the job was done, the hands were mustered aft. Nobby organised a firing party and there, on the tilting deck, the Captain read a short funeral service and they consigned their messmates to the deep. The funeral service was repeatedly interrupted by the helm orders that were being shouted from man to man along the deck. The thin 'Ashes to ashes' and the 'Dust to dust' for the dead were mingled with the harsh 'Midships' and 'Starboard thirty-five' of men who were holding on grimly to the precious life that had been spared them.

By now a small force of destroyers had gathered round the ship. Captain Mountbatten ordered them to take up an anti-aircraft and anti-submarine screen around the *Kelly*.

They were glad of friends when the bombers found them. On board the *Kelly*, even without power, they managed to put up a token barrage. 'Guns', now cooler than ice, organised the few men now available so that one gun's crew did the job of two. The guns were trained manually on to a rough bearing, and as soon as the Germans came within range the men, rushing from one mounting to another, would open fire. All the ready-use ammunition had been thrown overboard, but a volunteer party undertook the difficult and dangerous task of climbing in the dark down to the magazines to fetch up ammunition to fight the guns.

Food and fresh water were very scarce on board. A food hunt was organised but had no luck, until one of the boy seamen managed to squeeze through into the wrecked canteen. He crawled out with an enormous box of liquorice allsorts. Everyone immediately stuffed themselves with liquorice until their mouths refused to taste any more. Then came the consequence.

'The difference between all these bloody allsorts and a good dose of salts is about ten minutes. We *are* in action today all right,' said one sufferer.

For water they had to drink that out of the cooling jackets on the guns. It was filthy with grease and glycerine, but it *was* a drink and they were far too thirsty to be particular. George was thirsty, too, but like a good little matelot he shared the water in his dish.

George had been missing for some time after the explosion, until someone shouted, 'Where's George?' Instead of giving the usual answer, 'Gone to Lyons', they started to search for him. It was impossible to get for'ard through the canteen flat in the normal way, as the entire centre of the ship there was torn up and the quantities of oil swilling about made it fatally easy to fall through into the flooded space below. Eventually someone went over the top and, lowering himself down through the hole in the petty officers' mess, made his way for'ard. There George was found asleep in the hammock net.

By this time the weather had taken a decided turn for the worse and the tow had parted again. Captain Mountbatten had begun to notice the *Kelly*'s sluggish movements and recognised the imminent danger of capsizing. He calculated that he needed to remove at least ten tons of top-weight to preserve stability. Torpedoes, depth-charges, ammunition and boats had already been ditched and all that was left was the ship's company who were all huddled on the upper deck. They weighed in the aggregate more than ten tons, so he decided to transfer most of the men to the supporting ships and to call for volunteers to form a small party which would remain aboard.

While boats from the other ships were taking the men off the *Kelly,* the Germans bombed them, but a heavy anti- aircraft barrage from all the ships present drove them off.

The *Kelly* lay wallowing in the waves, waiting for the tug which was on its way to their assistance. The Captain then decided that with the ship in her present condition, and with the possibility of submarines being in the vicinity, it was not wise to remain aboard overnight. So, just before dusk, the six officers and twelve men who had stayed with the ship were taken off.

When they returned in the morning they found that one little matelot had stayed aboard. The cat Hawthorn had been in an interesting condition for some time now, and she stayed aboard that night to have her kittens in the drawer of the navigator's desk.

Soon the tug appeared and took them in tow.

'Where are we making for, sir?' they shouted.

'The Tyne,' answered Mountbatten, without a second's hesitation.

But the *Kelly* was now lower in the water than ever. Her motion grew steadily more sluggish, and she no longer rose to the waves.

'One foot in the grave,' they all thought.

Food and water were still the main items of interest aboard. All the fresh water had been contaminated by salt, and grub seemed to be entirely non-existent. However, Nobby Clarke detailed a 'scrounging party' to go and see what they could find. Nobby and the Chief E.R.A. went down into the gear-room and smashed the calorifier with a sledgehammer, getting a few gallons of water that way.

Meanwhile, someone went for'ard through the wreckage and got a huge leg of pork and other eatables from the smashed canteen store.

'Well, we're O.K. for eats now,' said Nobby.

Then the Germans paid them another visit. It may have been the sight of their temporary cook dashing to the nearest gun with his apron flying and a soup ladle in his hand that won the day, for after they had fired a few rounds the Germans made off 'without even dropping a curtsey', as someone said.

The sea was still choppy, and that night the tow parted again. They spent half the night getting rid of the broken tow-wire and getting a new one fitted. All the work had to be done by hand. Captain, officers and men heaved and strained on the greasy, lively wire until it was in place and once more they were under way and heading for home.

All this time the ship creaked and groaned under them. All they could do was to keep their fingers crossed and pray that the *Kelly* did not break in half after all their efforts and go to the bottom.

So it went on – that stubborn, hand-to-mouth struggle against two enemies, the human and the elemental. But at last, after they had been under tow for over ninety hours they sighted the mouth of the Tyne. As the procession slowly passed into the river mouth a great cheer went up from the people of Tyneside who had come out to welcome their ship home. As they passed down the river the news spread and all the shipyard workers knocked off work with one accord to come and give them a cheer, while at the same time all the ships in the river sounded their sirens and made a brave noise.

At first they were secured alongside a cruiser. Then the *Kelly* was taken into drydock at Hawthorn's. Her builders welcomed her with open arms, first as an old friend miraculously saved from the sea, and secondly as perhaps the greatest tribute to their workmanship that had ever been made.

When the water was drained from the drydock and the

full extent of the damage was seen everyone was astounded that she could have survived at all. Only her brilliant design and the splendid workmanship put into her by her builders had held her together. Mr Cole's adaption of the longitudinal system had been triumphantly vindicated. No other method would have prevented her from breaking in two. But it was a very near thing. Cole subsequently made calculations at the Admiralty and worked out that if the men had not been removed from the ship on that second night, the *Kelly* would, as her Captain had feared, have turned over.

It was subsequently rumoured that the King had wished Cole to receive a knighthood for his brilliant work on modern destroyer design but that he had not been considered senior enough in the Corps of Naval Constructors to receive the honour.

When the last bodies were removed from the wreckage and buried in Hebburn Cemetery, many thousands of the people of Tyneside came to pay tribute to the *Kelly*'s dead. At the head of their grave a tablet was placed which read,

> H.M.S. *Kelly*. In memory of the 27 men killed in action with E-boats off the German minefields in the night of 9th May, 1940. This memorial was erected by Officers and Men of the Ship and Workmen of Hebburn Shipbuilding Yard.

As the train taking the survivors on leave left Newcastle someone started to sing 'Has anybody here seen Kelly?' Everyone on the crowded station took it up, and in a corner of the crowd a small group started 'Will ye no come back again?'

CHAPTER VII

NEW BROOMS

REPAIRS this time were a big job. Survivors at home on leave told their relatives:

'First it was a new stern, then the bow got wiped, now they're putting a new midships section on her. She'll be a brand-new ship when they've finished with her this time.'

They were close to the truth. That torpedo had torn the guts out of the ship. Besides a new midships section, a new for'ard boiler-room and flanking bulkheads, all the compartments bordering on the wrecked part would need rebuilding and the bridge sagged like a bomb-torn house. The hole in the ship was so big that two double-decker buses could have been driven through it.

The midships section hung above the drydock bottom in a rigor mortis of torn and frantically twisted metal. From this wild graveyard a volunteer party of seamen and dockyard maties dragged the last bodies. It was not a pleasant task and it needed courage to do it.

had its hands full with war. There wasn't a single matelot anywhere in the world who wasn't chokka to the eyebrows. Into this happy state of affairs steamed the *Kelly* as the month of December dawned.

Aboard the *Warspite,* Admiral Cunningham's flagship, was young Petty Officer Smith, a yeoman of signals. He served aboard the *Warspite* for two and a half years in all and saw plenty of action in her. He was at the Second Battle of Narvik when Vice-Admiral Whitworth flew his flag in her and led the British squadron up Ofot Fiord: *Warspite*; four destroyers from the 'pre-war' flotillas, *Icarus, Hero, Foxhound,* and *Forester*; four Tribals, *Cossack, Bedouin, Punjabi* and *Eskimo;* and one destroyer from the Fighting Fifth, the *Kimberley,* which ably represented the flotilla while her leader lay under repairs in the London Graving Dock and took a big part in the sinking of the six German destroyers. Smith remembered that grim northern battle in the rain, when the *Warspite* chased a different enemy under a very different sky some months later.

On a bright, blue afternoon in the Ionian Sea, not far from the toe of the Italian mainland, Smith was on the bridge, when he took a signal from the cruiser *Neptune* which no British Commander-in-Chief in the Mediterranean had received for nearly a hundred and fifty years. The signal read:

'Enemy battle fleet in sight.'

Once it might have been Nelson receiving the signal. Now it was Cunningham. That the Fleet was able to do no more than damage the Italian battleship *Cesare* was due to the fact that the Fascists built their ships to run, not to fight.

When eventually he got his relief, Smith went back to the United Kingdom wondering what his next job would be. His anxiety was short-lived. When he returned to barracks from his foreign-service leave he found himself in great demand at the Drafting Office.

'Hello, what now?' he thought, as he walked through the drill shed. 'Another battler, I shouldn't wonder. More bull, more pusser routine, collar and tie on watch, the lot!'

But he was wrong, and the Drafting Master-at-Arms soon corrected him.

'You've got a bit of all right there, mate,' he said; 'you've drawn the *Kelly* – Mountbatten.'

Mountbatten! Lord Louis! *Kelly,* flotilla leader of D.5! But what shook Smith most was the thought that he, a young yeoman of signals of only three years' seniority, would be under the eye of a captain who knew his signals better than anyone in the Fleet. Smith knew as well as any other responsible member of his profession how Mountbatten's record stood in that respect. His misgivings would not have been allayed if he could have been present on the *Kelly*'s bridge on her first commission, during one of those off-the-record sessions when Mountbatten would race his own Signals Officer in the sending and receiving of morse, with each man performing at the rate of thirty words per minute.

'Oh, well,' he thought, 'if it isn't this one it'll be something worse.'

Six months had passed since the *Kelly* crawled up the Tyne and went, first to Palmer's Yard, where between them the cruiser *Newcastle* and the giant crane *Titan II* held her up, and then to Hawthorn's. One of the men who watched the slow procession up-stream and downed tools to give the ship a cheer was Bill Marshall. Bill was a boilermaker, and on that day he was working on board the submarine depot ship *Titania,* which was in the Tyne herself for repairs. He turned to his workmate.

'She looks more like a submarine than a destroyer,' he said. 'I wonder what they must feel like.'

A civilian's remark, perhaps, but Bill Marshall's time as

a civilian was running short at that very moment, did he but know it. On July 31st he was called up, and on November 14th he found himself, a very new engine-room artificer, standing on the deck of the ship he had gazed and wondered at six months before, a member of her ship's company. He did not have long to wait to find out what they had felt like. He discovered that there were many men from the *Kelly*'s first commission aboard her, men like Gordon Rogers, who had been taken on to Mountbatten's staff as a telephone operator when the headquarters of the Fifth Flotilla had been moved to Immingham during the months while the *Kelly* was repairing.

The *Kelly* was famous by now. Wherever you went the name would come up sooner or later and someone would say:

'Kelly? Oh, you want to steer clear of her, mate – she's always in trouble, she is. You might get a medal, and on the other hand you might be digging a hole in the 'ogwash.'

Wherever such sentiments were aired, the general opinion seemed to be that if you were 'all for it' then the *Kelly* was the ship for you, but if you had your head screwed on the right way you followed the old rule, which is widely preached in the Navy but which surprisingly few ever seemed to practice, namely, 'Never volunteer for anything.'

Then a notice appeared in the drill shed, asking all ex-*Kelly* men to volunteer for her next commission. This invitation came from Captain Mountbatten, who wanted to start the new commission with as many old and tried hands as possible. Half an hour after the notice had gone up the queue stretched half-way across the drill shed and back again. *Never volunteer for anything.*

Young 'Rock' Wilkins saw that notice. He was a cockney from Camden Town, a keen young matelot and a member of the R.N.V.R. Rocky was an anti-aircraft rating. He had just qualified as an A.A.3 and had a nice, quiet little number as P.T.I.s' messman.

Your Physical Training Instructor was a hard, hard man, especially in the swimming-bath. If you could swim, if you could pass your swimming test, you had no worries and that chlorinated torture-chamber held no terrors for you. But if you could not, you faced long, miserable hours of choking in green, chlorinated water, with your instructor exhorting you from the side. In his hands he would hold a long pole. Holding it six inches in front of your nose, he wheedled you on with a hoarse:

'Come on, lad – just another two strokes. You can do it.'

Rocky Wilkins had been through all this, though nobody had managed to make him do more than a dog-paddle. However, he was on the right side of the fence now. He found that, on the whole, the P.T.I.s weren't such a bad lot. What was more to the point, they had to keep fit, so they did not drink their tots, and Rocky and his fellow messmen did very well out of them. Then, one day, one of the P.T.I.s came into the mess, just before dinner.

'They're auctioneering the *Kelly*'s effects over in the drill shed this afternoon,' he announced. If he had expected the roof to fall in he was disappointed. There was a pause.

'Well,' he said, 'don't knock me down in the rush.'

'Well – er – I mean . . . it's *dead* men's effects, isn't it, P.O.?' said Rocky awkwardly.

'You H.O.s make me spit! What's wrong with dead men's gear? Them that owned that gear were *men,* sonny boy, and they got the 'ammer fighting for stupid, 'alf-'ard bastards like you. You ought to be proud to wear some of their gear.'

Wilkins thought about that for a while. Eventually he did go over to the drill shed. By the time he got there nearly everything had gone. There was no clothing left, but he managed to get a ditty box, a handsome thing of polished wood. He was walking back through the drill shed, when he saw a group of men standing round the drafting noticeboards. He went over to see what the big attraction was and found that it was a notice addressed to all ex-members of the ship's company of H.M.S. *Kelly* to come forward and volunteer for her new commission, which was about to begin. The notice was signed, 'Louis Mountbatten, Captain, Royal Navy.'

He'd heard about Mountbatten. In his mind he was a vague and legendary figure – a bit like Nelson, almost.

'The *Kelly* – what sort of ship is that?' he asked the nearest matelot.

'*Kelly*? Best ship in the Andrew, mate, that's all,' said the man, 'and I ought to know.'

'Why, were you on the *Kelly*, then?' asked Rocky.

'Not flippin' many,' said the other, 'and I'm going back on 'er toot sweet an' all. Best ship in the Andrew *and* the best skipper.' Then he noticed the ditty box under Wilkins's arm. 'You get that from *Kelly*'s effects?'

'Yes,' said Rocky, 'I just got it. Couldn't get any clobber – just this.'

'Well, you got a good bargain there, mate,' said the *Kelly* man. ' 'ere, let's 'ave a butcher's inside it.'

Wilkins opened the lid. Inside was the name 'Cave, Stoker First Class'.

'Cave,' said the *Kelly* man, 'Cave. No, I don't remember him. Anyway, it's yours now, mate; you've taken over.'

All the way back to the mess that remark kept hammering at his mind. Another voice kept saying, 'It's yours now, mate; you've taken over.' Wilkins thought so hard that he forgot to take it on the double across the parade-ground and got a bottle from the 'Gestapo'. He looked at the box under his arm. He felt that he was carrying a part of the *Kelly* with him, that he'd got some sort of interest in the ship now. He did not feel that he had bought the box for his own, but rather that its rightful owner had loaned it to him for safe keeping. *It's yours now, mate.* He felt that he had almost stepped into the dead man's shoes, taking his gear like that. It was practically asking him to join.

He was still frowning and deep in thought when he got back to the mess. Old Lofty, his oppo, noticed the furrowed brow.

'Hello, what's up with you, Wings?' he asked.

'Who, me? Nothing, mate,' said Wilkins. He paused. 'Lofty, have you seen that notice up in the drill shed?'

'About the *Kelly*? Yeah, I seen it. What about it?' said Lofty. 'You 'aven't gone and fallen for that load of flannel, 'ave you?'

'Me? No! Big ships meself, Lofty boy,' said Rocky with a bit of bluster. But Lofty didn't like the look on his face.

'There's one thing you got to learn in the Andrew, mate.' he said. 'Never volunteer for anything.'

So Rocky went and volunteered. When he said, 'I've come to volunteer for the *Kelly*,' the Drafting Master-at Arms said:

'You'll have to wait in the queue, son.'

And the very first bloke he met in the queue was old Lofty.

'Lofty' Howarth joined R.N.B. after service in the cruiser *Calcutta* and did a short gunnery course. After that the biggest problem was to keep out of the clutches of the 'Gestapo', the barrack guard. But in order to loaf successfully in Chatham you had to have your wits about you. Lofty's class, which naturally enough had stuck together when they came into main barracks from the Gunnery School, did this very successfully by marching round as if they were an organised party. They even had a 'class leader', with a supposedly official chit in his hand. This little scrap of paper worked miracles, and the Gestapo never worried them. They stopped at all the heads for a quiet burn, though never too long to be suspicious, and at times, during working hours, a strategic withdrawal to the Tunnel proved effective. In this way they kept out of trouble.

All the time drafts were flying round them like leaves in the wind. Eventually Howarth's oppo collected a draft to the *Kelly*. He said to Lofty: 'Come down and see if you can volunteer.' Down he went, found that another man on the *Kelly* draft had gone sick, and took his place. Of his original class on the Q.R.3 course three were going to the *Kelly*. They were all proud as peacocks.

Of course they didn't say so.

'It's a ruddy pierhead jump,' they dripped. 'I've been shanghaied.'

Petty Officer Ted West was Nobby Clarke's successor. West had returned to England in August, after a long spell is one of the 'white sepulchres', the County-class cruiser *Cornwall*. The Admiralty lost no time in packing him off to Whale Island, that mint of gunners, where he did a higher gunnery course, specialising in anti-aircraft weapons. Back in Chatham he was assigned to the Gunnery School as an instructor, while awaiting draft to a sea-going ship.

Each day, hundreds of names would go up on the drafting notice-boards, and all the men in depot who knew they were due for a ship scanned the long columns, looking for their names. The day arrived when West saw his name down, alongside H.M.S. *Kelly*. He was very pleased to have caught a destroyer, though he had been out of England a long time and knew nothing about the *Kelly*. The censorship had prevented him from learning anything about her epic in the North Sea.

But besides the Active Service men, all of whom had signed on in the Navy for periods of five, seven or twelve years, there was a new brand of sailors in barracks.

The Navy was expanding beyond all imagination now. Thousands of men were needed, especially for the man-

10

ning of the new corvettes and destroyers coming into service. These the small and now sadly depleted ranks of regulars could not supply, so the 'Hostilities Only' rating was born.

Young Taff Davies did his training at H.M.S. *Raleigh* before joining R.N.B. Chatham. He hadn't been there long, when he came into the mess one day and found a draft chit waiting for him on the shelf.

'What ship, mate?' asked a bearded, three-badge able seaman.

'*Kelly*,' said Taff, who had never heard the name before.

'*Kelly!*' said Stripey. 'Ha, you've caught a packet there, mate – that's Mountbatten's ship. Proper death-or-glory boy he is.'

Taff was a young country lad, away from home for the first time, and his heart hit the deck at these words and the way they were spoken. Then he got draft leave and went home. His mother opened the door.

'I know, you've got a ship,' she said at once in a miserable voice.

'Yes, mam,' said Taff. 'I'm going on the *Kelly* with Lord Louis Mountbatten.'

Immediately his mother's face lit up.

'Oh, I am relieved,' she said, as she closed the door behind him. 'He's the first cousin of the King, and those people are never allowed to take any chances.'

The ship's company fell in in the drill shed late one cold November afternoon. There, amidst the piles of bags and hammocks, old *Kelly* men met new. Those who knew nothing of the ship's history were quickly put in the picture by the old hands, who were going back for another dose of 'Mountbatten medicine'. They left barracks about five o'clock and boarded the train for London. When they got to The Smoke they found they had several hours to kill before they could catch their Newcastle train at King's Cross. They had all worked up a thirst by that time. 'Let's go and have a wet,' said someone. Oddly enough this idea seemed popular, so the draft split up into groups and proceeded to do a crawl of the pubs in the King's Cross area. They had quite a merry evening, all the merrier for being unexpected.

So congenial a time was had by all, in fact, that one party almost missed the connection altogether. They rushed into the station and on to the nearest platform.

'Come on, lads, pile in,' shouted someone; 'this is the one.'

But it wasn't. It was going to Newcastle all right, but the Navy does not take kindly to matelots proceeding independently to their far-flung destinations, and the main draft was on another train. However, they arrived at Hebburn next morning about the same time as the remainder of the draft and got off with a 'bottle'.

On the first day of December Captain Mountbatten rejoined the *Kelly*. By now he had had two mounts shot under him. Only two days before he joined his old ship he had brought the destroyer *Javelin* into Plymouth – the *Javelin*, or what was left of her, after the Germans had blown off her bow and stern. Now he was in the saddle again.

When he examined the lists of his new ship's company he was staggered and seriously perturbed to find that, out of two hundred and sixty men, one hundred and seventy were 'Hostilities Only' ratings, none of whom had ever been to sea before, much less been in action. He cleared lower deck and in his introductory speech told the new men that he was not satisfied with the very large number of untrained, inexperienced men that Chatham had thought fit to send him. Aboard the *Kelly*, he told them, he wanted only real sailors who knew their jobs. This was a warning and the H.O.s took it.

No one was keener to make good than young Rocky Wilkins. As a peacetime member of the R.N.V.R., he had already gone far towards proving that. One morning, a few days after Captain Mountbatten had issued his warning to the new men, Rocky was sipping a mug of hot tea during stand-easy, when a man came into the mess flourishing a copy of the *Daily Mirror*.

'Some of you H.O.s want to read this,' he said, and flung the paper open at the centre page. 'That'll show you what you've got to live up to!'

'Let's have a dekko,' said Rocky. He spread the paper out on the table and read:

Torpedo, Bombs, Fog and Storm

BRITISH GRIT IN A BRITISH SHIP
BEATS THE LOT

It was there, the story of that stubborn fight across the North Sea, that grim action fought seven months before, when Rocky and so many others in the *Kelly*'s new ship's company had still been cocksure stroppy-Jacks in training. A few more of the new hands gathered round and gaped over Rocky's shoulder.

What they read was a vivid account of an event which, until now, they had only been able to piece together from scraps of reminiscence thrown to them by some of the men who had been on the spot. They read:

> Lord Louis Mountbatten, cousin of the King, refused to abandon and sink his ship, H.M.S. *Kelly,* when she was crippled by a German torpedo off the enemy coast.
>
> Instead, he and his crew, fighting with the faith and fire of Nelson, used the destroyer as a floating fence to sink a hunted Nazi torpedo-boat – then defied enemy bombing attacks for three days and made port safely.

'That's *this* ship,' each man said to himself, '*my* ship.' Alongside the story was a picture of the *Kelly* as she was when she moved, crippled, down the Tyne, her upper decks awash and the gap yawning along her starboard side where the E-boat had swept away boats and davits. They read on:

> But today, *Kelly*, her wounds healed, after seven months in hospital, is in active service again waiting for the Germans to come out and fight.

'And that's us,' they told themselves, and went away more resolved than ever to live up to the example their shipmates had already set them.

A paragraph further down the page caught Wilkins's eye. It said:

> A naval rating, First Class Stoker Cave, was severely injured.
>
> 'Never mind me, Doc,' he told a sick-berth attendant; 'I'm done for. Help the other lads – but hold me when I die. I'll tell you when.'

Stoker Cave – the name on his ditty box. The scene in the drill shed at Chatham came back into his mind, and the words someone had said to him then. *It's yours now, mate; you've taken over.*

'Yes, I've taken over now,' he said to himself, 'and I won't let you down.'

If any man, in his moments of self-doubt, had fears that the future might prove too heavy for him to bear, there was now a new source added to the *Kelly*'s strength to which he could turn for help and guidance. This source lay in the personality of the ship's new First Lieutenant.

Lord Hugh Beresford was the third son of the Marquess of Waterford and the great nephew of Admiral Lord Charles Beresford, the famous sailor who had been Commander-in-Chief, Mediterranean, thirty-five years earlier.

His family line was long and distinguished. An ancestor, Thomas Beresford, had fought at Agincourt, and throughout the long and troubled centuries his family had continued to bear arms in defence of their country.

But to Hugh Beresford the call to arms in his chosen profession meant more than a mere defence of home and country. To him it was almost a crusade. For he was a man worth the name of Christian, a preaching and a practising Christian gentleman, who saw the war quite clearly as a conflict of right against wrong, who recognised that a Christian's path lay through the heart of the violence and was thus, in his own case, constant with his path of duty as a naval officer, sworn to defend King and Country. Indeed, he saw the Royal Navy as a great potential apostle of Christian law and order, and in the uneasy days of a false peace had deliberately chosen to remain in the Navy among the hardships of destroyer life, when he could have retired to a life of ease and comfort ashore. So certain was he that he, his professional skills and, above all, his faith would soon be needed.

He was a shy man by nature, quiet in manner, with nothing of the natural mixer in him. Nevertheless, like Mountbatten, he was universally liked. One of the men who had worked on the ship while she was refitting wrote of him: 'The chief impression he left on the working men here was of a lovable personality, who lived above the distinctions of class and creed.'

He knew fear. He had faced it and fought with it many times.

'The worst part of fear,' he would often say, 'whether it is of meeting people or of the dentist's drill or of bombs, is anticipation. My new faith in God has not prevented me from feeling fear; but I have found that God lifts fear from those who start by admitting they are frightened. I have learnt to be honest about my fears with another officer on the bridge or with the man who happens to be next to me. That opens the way of God to take charge again.

What is more, it often helps the other fellow to get rid of his own fears.'

This was the officer the men of the *Kelly* would now be responsible to. This was the man who would superintend their daily life and work. Next to their Captain, this was the man to whom they would entrust their lives.

CHAPTER VIII

HOSTILITIES ONLY

CHRISTMAS was coming and the geese were getting fat. Aboard the *Kelly* special shore leave was given to all mess caterers.

Lofty Howarth had been made caterer of his mess. A whip round among the twenty men in the mess plus an allowance by the Canteen Committee gave him about seven pounds to buy all the extras for a jovial Christmas. He took the money and went off into 'Canny Newcassel'.

He managed to get some peel, raisins and most of the pudding ingredients and began to feel he had accomplished something. Then he started looking for a turkey. Turkeys, pork and chickens were on show in plenty. But they were all booked.

'The civvies have bagged the lot,' dripped Lofty.

About five o'clock he had just about become resigned to the idea of a bit of pusser's beef for Christmas dinner, when his luck changed. Lofty happened to be wearing a cap tally with the name of his old ship on it, H.M.S. *Calcutta.* At this stage in the war to have a ship's name on your cap instead of the plain 'H.M.S.' was highly illegal, but, illegal or not, this time it did the Navy a bit of good. He was walking through Grainger Street Market, feeling that he had definitely let his messmates down, when he spotted a butcher's shop which he had missed. He went inside.

'Any turkeys, mate?' asked Lofty hopefully.

'Sorry, chum; they're all bought,' said the manager with an apologetic grin.

'Chickens, then, or a bit of pork?' tried Lofty again.

But it was the same story. He was just walking out of the shop, when there was a shout from behind him.

'Are you from the *Calcutta*?'

Lofty turned round just as one of the shop assistants rushed up to him. He found his hand being pumped up and down.

'Yes, that's right,' he said, 'least I was.'

'Don't you remember me?' asked the man. Lofty squinted at him.

'No, I'm afraid I don't, mate,' he said. 'Were you in the Andrew then?'

'No, I was in the army and the *Calcutta* picked me up from Dunkirk,' said the now very excited man. 'Saved my flaming life you blokes did. Small world, eh?'

'Yes,' said Lofty, 'with a lot of turkeys in it, and none of them for us.'

'Oh well, we'll soon see about that,' said the manager.

When Lofty left the shop he was the better off for a huge lump of pork and a turkey. Back in the mess, he was the hero of the hour.

There was one big Christmas-box everyone on board could look forward to – a working-up party in Scapa Flow. With all those green hands aboard that was one thing the ship needed plenty of.

Already there was a good spirit aboard ship, stemming

from the old hands and from the determination of the new men to be worthy of a fine and famous ship.

'Life is grand with me,' wrote Beresford. 'I have got a far clearer vision than ever before of how to run a ship under God's orders. Even though a number of people on board do not realise the fact, the ship is none the less God's, and I have a strong feeling that our success or failure during these coming months depends directly on my listening to Him and following out His instructions calmly and coolly.'

They finally sailed on December 15th. Once out at sea, the rails were soon crowded with groaning men, their faces ghastly with seasickness. The *Kelly* rolled and pitched wildly, burying her bull-ring in every sea.

Some of them recovered quickly, but many were still suffering, when, suddenly, after nightfall, gunfire was sighted on the horizon.

Mountbatten's first thought was that the flashes must be coming from British ships at gunnery practice. They were surely too near the English coast to be German warships. On the other hand, he had just come from a night action with the rest of the flotilla which had started in precisely this way. Quickly he and his staff examined the flotilla exercise programmes and the information which had been issued to them for their trip to Scapa. There were no British ships scheduled to hold gunnery practice in the area that night. The gunfire must be from German destroyers attacking our coastal shipping.

Swiftly the Captain weighed the situation. His ship had not been worked up. The greater majority of the ship's company had never been to sea before and many were still prostrate with seasickness. If the *Kelly,* with a sick and untrained crew, deliberately sought action with the enemy she ran a grave risk of being sunk.

But in his recommissioning speech Mountbatten had told them that he would always go hard for the enemy, that he would fight to the last, that he would never abandon ship. What if he now abandoned the chance of action? 'Always steer towards the sound of the guns,' he had said, and the buzz that this was the enemy had already spread through the ship like wildfire. If he turned away now the whole effect of his words would be lost, the morale of this green crew would sink to zero.

So he accepted the risk. The *Kelly* turned and steered for the flashes. Down below in the engine-room the new hands were doing their utmost to get as much speed as possible out of the ship. The sharp turn threw one of them down on the floorplates.

'Oh, you'll have to do better than that, mate,' said Leading Stoker Webber. 'That's one of Louis' best party tricks, only he usually does it when you're in the mess drinking soup.'

Indeed, it was old hands like Webber who carried the day. The experienced men worked feverishly, doing in minutes what it would normally have taken weeks of drill to do, showing the new hands exactly what to do if the next few minutes found them in action for the first time.

In fact, if enthusiasm means anything they might have given a very good account of themselves. But the gunfire at the last minute turned out to be friendly. A destroyer had been given special permission to hold night practice, and the *Kelly* had not been informed.

The effect on morale, however, was tremendous. The Captain had taken them at full speed towards the guns. He had shown them what 'Keep On' meant. It was a happier and a more efficient ship that resumed her interrupted trip to Scapa.

Ted West went back to his labours on the messdecks. He tried hard to remember that hardly any of these youngsters had ever seen a messdeck before and forced himself to recollect his own early days at sea.

These had been spent aboard the old, coal-burning battleship, the *Emperor of India,* which he had joined in 1926. She was a member of the old Third Battle Squadron then, along with the *Marlborough, Benbow* and the *Iron Duke.* He would be seeing the *Iron Duke* again very shortly – lying in shallow water on the bottom of Scapa Flow, where Jerry had put her last year. After his training in the stone frigate *Ganges,* at Ipswich, the messdeck of the old *Emperor* was a strange and frightening place. He tried hard, therefore, to imagine what it must be like for the men he found under his care now.

Most of them had to be taught the rudiments of cooking or, rather, the preparation of food for cooking. In destroyers each mess is responsible for the preparation of their own meals. They then take the food to the galley, where cookie sees that it goes into the oven, marked with the tally of the mess it comes from, and is properly done. Most of the dishes thus produced are best left to the imagination.

West had to supervise all this, showing bewildered and rebellious ex-civilians, used to a quick snack at Lyons, how to mix pastry, how to peel potatoes and hang them up in the fanny in water, how to dress the meat and make good navy tea. He had to superintend the arrangement of rotas for cooks of the messes, making sure that every man did his full twenty-four hours on duty, from washing up after one evening meal to dishing up the next. He watched over them when they scrubbed out in the mornings and, like Nobby, his predecessor, often found himself on his hands and knees showing them how. Then, the mess spick and span, he had to hand over the cooks to his colleagues on the upper decks, when 'Cooks of the mess fall in' was piped half-way through the forenoon. With them away working part of ship again he would get his messdeck sweepers to give the hammock nets a good square off, winkle the last loafers out of their funk-holes and look forward to 'Up spirits' and his tot.

At times his unpopularity was to get him down. It all started when he warned the men that it was not quite the thing to leave their hammocks slung after the hands had been called. He made it quite clear that the owner of any hammock left up after the hands had been mustered in future would be taken aft and put straight in the rattle. The morning after he had made this announcement, after both watches had fallen in, he took the names of sixteen men who had disregarded the warning, and they were each given five days' slack hammock drill by the First Lieutenant.

'But, you know,' said Ted sadly to his cronies in the petty officers' mess, 'there's no justice in this world. *I* have to turn out one hour before the rest of the hands to muster the offenders when they bring their hammocks aft to be inspected.'

When they steamed into Scapa Flow they all looked a good deal more like a ship's company than they had done out in the open sea. Most of the sprog seamen had conquered their stomachs by now and were getting to know their way round the ship.

Mr Churchill had been present when the Flow was opened again for business back in March, and the Germans had welcomed the Home Fleet back to its ancestral hearth by filling the channel they had planned to use with magnetic mines. In fact, the First Lord was forced to transfer from the flagship *Nelson* to a destroyer and creep humbly into the Flow through Switha Sound, 'the tradesman's entrance'.

At Scapa the Kellys went straight into their working-up exercises. When they first used their armament history was repeated. Scapa at that time was a prohibited area for aircraft. On this particular day Ted West was on deck, when he suddenly heard the sound of ack-ack fire. Although they had had no air-raid warning, they immediately closed up at the guns. Suddenly West spotted an aircraft coming low over the harbour. He could not identify the type, so, as it had obviously been fired on already, he did not hesitate but started blazing away with his quadruple point fives. His first burst was so close to the target that the pilot sheered off in a hurry and dropped his recognition flares.

'Well, it taught him where the prohibited area was, anyway,' said Ted.

They went through all the normal trials, sub-calibre and full-calibre shoots, night-encounter exercises and the rest, and in between managed to get an occasional run ashore to the canteen. Here the beer was rationed by the issuing of special beer tickets. One man got three tickets and after that went thirsty, unless he could get in on the brisk little trade that flourished in these coupons.

One day the seamen were practising manning the whaler at the davits as sea-boats' crews, being lowered and pulling away to recover a lifebuoy thrown into the water. To the great disgust of the First Lieutenant five successive crews took between four and five minutes to accomplish this, and when the Captain came on deck he reported that they were exceptionally slow. Mountbatten immediately called for a volunteer crew of officers, with officers as sea-boat lowerers and himself as stroke oar. They manned the boat; it was lowered, they cast off and pulled over to the lifebuoy and back in less than a minute and a half. They were received with hearty cheers by the ship's company.

Down in the engine-room there was a new bunch of stokers.

'Not so good as the old mob,' said Webber, upper-deck killick and Chief Stoker's right-hand man, who had a big share in licking the new men into shape. But one man at least they could rely on.

Scouse Rogers still had his 'uke' with him, to help build up morale on the messdeck. He found an enthusiastic audience for his songs and soon exhausted his repertoire. 'The Chief Stoker's Lament' was an even greater favourite this time. The O.D. stokers soon learned the words, which Rogers had to repeat ad nauseam.

Now we have a chief stoker who's not very tall,
He comes down and shakes us and gives us a call.
'Come on now my hearties, get lashed up and stow,
Get your flippin' breakfast and get down below.'

Then the sprogs would join in the chorus:

Side, side, Kelly's *ship's side, Jimmy looks on it with pride,*
He'd have a blue fit if he saw someone spit
On the side of the Kelly's *ship's side.*

When they thought he had finished he rounded off the song, and the recital, with:

Down in the stokehold, it's not very deep,
A second-class stoker is having a sleep.
Do not shake him oh Chiefie, but just let him rest,
For that second-class stoker's been doing his best.

And that was about the truth of it. They *were* doing their best, even if leave was a thing of the past. The young ones could not quite get rid of those glamorous dreams in which a matelot's life was spent in a brand-new tiddley suit with at least two girls on each arm. Scapa and working up didn't quite fit in, somehow.

Then, one day, they put to sea in a hurry.

'There goes the *Daily Mirror* boat,' said all the big ships.

The buzz said that they were going south again, but this time it was wide of the mark, for they turned north into choppy grey seas, and the compass needle swung towards the Arctic. 'It's the Shetlands again, then,' was the buzz's answer, as Start Point, then North Ronaldsay, dropped astern. Wrong again.

'I'll tell you lads what we're going to do. We're going up to Reykjavik and try our hand at squaring the Arctic

Circle,' was one petty officer's answer to the problem. 'We'll probably be picking up a party of Commandos and dropping 'em on the Norwegian coast for a bash at Jerry.' This was certainly the most imaginative guess of all, for one very good reason.

That the Germans held the Norwegian ports had been bad enough, with the Nazi navy firmly established in Bergen and Trondheim, but if they had ever succeeded in occupying Iceland the routing of our convoys through northern waters would have become impossible. Here, at least, we beat the Germans to the punch. On the very day that Hitler gave the order which sent his armies into Belgium and Holland the Royal Marines landed at Reykjavik, the Icelandic capital, and soon the whole island had been occupied. It would be a splendidly situated base for aircraft patrols, while convoy escorts would be able to use it as a fuelling stop.

So, one mark for trying. For the guess was wrong. They were heading in the direction of Iceland all right, but they stopped off half-way, at the Faroes. All right, then, a spot of shore leave, anyway. Sorry, lads; this is a business trip, even if it is Christmas Eve tomorrow.

With all those turkeys, plum puddings and various bits of Christmas fare on board, they were all looking forward to a slap-up Christmas dinner and a Christmas Day to remember in the weary months ahead.

They had a Christmas Day to remember all right. Just as cooks of the mess were rolling up their sleeves and getting out the basin for mixing the ingredients (Lofty Howarth had even bought a new one for the occasion) a pipe sent them all away to their stations, and the *Kelly* made one of her 'so saying she swep' out' departures.

They got a contact and made the sea around it boil with depth charges. In a few minutes they sighted oil on the surface. They got back to the Faroes in darkness.

'Oh well, it'll be Christmas dinner on Boxing Day this year,' they said.

Boxing Day dawned. Christmas dinner? Not a bit of it. Just another U-boat hunt.

But the great day came at last. All the messes turned to with incredible speed and energy that forenoon in keen anticipation of the feast to come.

Lofty Howarth, naturally enough, was still in charge of the pudding operations in his mess, though he had many willing helpers, and altogether there were far too many cooks. Theirs was the only mess that had taken a chance on buying the ingredients and mixing the pudding themselves. Almost everything went into that pudding, including every single man's tot of bubbly. Eventually the chef accepted it.

When it reached the table Lofty took the awning off it. It looked wonderful, rich, ripe and fruity. You could smell the rum on the quarterdeck. Plates were laid out and rum-sauce was fetched from the galley. Then Lofty took up the knife. Amidst a breathless silence he took the first cut.

It was as hard as a rock.

The silence persisted and grew deeper. Then: 'Seen off again,' said Lofty savagely.

Pandemonium.

'Where's that bloody chef?' shouted everyone, cheered on by all the other messes, who were having the laugh of their lives.

'Request to state a complaint!'

Then they all turned on Lofty.

'What the hell did you do with it? You're a bloody fine caterer!'

Lofty was as wild as they were. 'And you're the best bastard to take over the books,' he shouted. 'I've resigned!' Anyone would have thrown a temperament in that spot.

Later they found out what had happened. An O.D. chef had put the pudding in the steamer and forgotten to add water to it. The pud had thus come out like petrified lava. Lofty never lived it down.

The fatal pudding stayed in the dish for a while.

'Ought to nail it to the mast-'ead as a warning,' said one man.

'Couldn't get a nail through it,' said another.

Nevertheless they all enjoyed that Christmas, each in his own way. Beresford noted:

'This has been a wonderful Christmas for me – a daily and often hourly thrill. I was left in charge of the ship for several days, and at the first Sunday prayers my guidance was, first, to read the following prayer, and then to tell the ship's company what I felt we are fighting for and ask God to bless the ship and us to His service.'

This was the prayer he read:

'O God, our loving Father, bless our efforts to make this ship efficient for your service. Help us to keep in mind the real causes of this war – dishonesty, greed, selfishness and lack of love – and to drive them out of this ship, so that she may be a pattern of the New World for which we are fighting. Bless also our homes and families. Give us the experience that there is no distance which cannot be bridged by your Holy Spirit if we open our hearts.'

Some time after Christmas one man received a parcel from home. The parcel had been some time in the post and the chicken that was in it was so high that it went straight through the porthole. In the letter that came with the parcel the lucky man's wife said that she particularly hoped they would enjoy the stuffing. It was not until several weeks afterwards that they discovered the 'stuffing' to have been a bottle of Scotch.

Seen off again! But, back in Scapa once more, there were compensations. One day 'Putty', the ship's painter, was painting the side at just about deck level, when he looked up and saw a sailor's dream of heaven. Next day, ashore in the canteen, he told some of his oppos from a chummy ship about it.

'I was slapping crab fat on the side,' he said, 'when all

of a sudden I looked up and saw a smashing blonde party coming across the deck.'

The 'smashing blonde party' was Frances Day, come to do a bit of morale building for the navy. She made a wonderful job of it and the Kellys never forgot her. That night she sang to them in the for'ard messdeck. At the end of her act she sang:

> I'm just a little bit light in the head,
> Me and my dog, we haven't been to bed,
> We went for a stroll, and we lost ourselves instead.
> Won't some *kind* gentleman see us home?

That was too much for the Kellys. The air was blue with wolf calls and those long, low whistles. This reception was coldly received – by the officers. But as for the lady . . . does any 'party' as 'smashing' as Miss Day ever really object to such a tribute?

Although the O.D.s were settling down a bit now, they still had much to learn.

One day they were doing an anti-submarine sweep from Scapa in company with another destroyer and were zig-zagging. Taff Davies and another O.D. were in the bulge on the starboard side of the bridge, on lookout duty. Taff's duty was to watch one quarter of the compass, from ninety degrees to dead astern, thus taking over where his oppo left off, who had the sector from bows to beam. The other was seasick and in no fit state to keep a very keen watch. After a while he nudged Taff quite casually in the ribs and said:

'Taff, is that a ship out there?'

Taff took one look and shouted at the top of his voice:

'Ship on the starboard bow!'

The officer of the watch immediately ordered a change of course and speed to investigate the sighting, and the Captain rushed to the bridge just in time to hear the starboard lookout getting a severe ticking off for not reporting the ship sooner. The strange ship turned out to be friendly, but when they got back to Scapa the Captain complimented the engine-room staff on their quick response to the orders from the bridge. Taff felt a bit hurt at being left out. After all, it wasn't his job to look out for'ard.

A short time after that he had another shock. This time the for'ard lookout was on form and he suddenly sighted a dim smudge of smoke on the horizon. He wasn't going to miss this one.

'Ship bearing green two-O!' he shouted, for all the ship to hear and the mermaids harping down below. The Captain ordered the challenge to be made as soon as the ship showed. The same time as the *Kelly* challenged the distant vessel she was challenged herself. They answered '*Kelly*' and the other answered '*Hood*'.

'I wonder what would have happened to us if they had opened fire first and challenged afterwards,' said Taff.

Apart from the frequent rushes to sea on U-boat hunts, things went on in the way a ship's routine usually does when she is not actually engaged on any particular operation – drills, spit and polish, shore leave when they could get it, and, above all, particularly for the sorely-tried Petty Officer West, seeing to the cleanliness and proper running of the messdecks. By hard work, persuasion and the help of the old hands he was beginning to make the rookie sailors houseproud, and things were beginning to run fairly smoothly.

The worst part of his job came when they returned to harbour. Invariably after a spell at sea the messdecks got flooded with water, and after constant watchkeeping (at times they were closed up at action stations all night) the men would flop down when and wherever they could. But West made it a firm rule that, before anyone relaxed, the messdecks should be dried out, cleaned and thoroughly ventilated, all wet clothing being hung up to dry. After a while the new hands got it into their still landlubberly heads that all this was only being done for their own good, and the petty officer of the messdecks became less unpopular. West himself was relieved at the change of attitude, because at heart he was anything but the brute he must have seemed.

By the New Year the Admiralty had evidently decided that the *Kelly* had had as much of a shake-down as they could allow her, for at the end of the first week of 1941 she left Scapa and went through Pentland Firth, westbound. That was January 7th. On the following day she came to the buoy at Greenock. They had two days there, time for one run ashore for each watch. Leave in a big city was doubly welcome after the wilds of the Orkneys and Faroes. In Glasgow they utterly disproved the Sassenach gibe at the meanness of Scotsmen. Where else in Great Britain could a serviceman find unlimited bus travel for the sum of a penny?

But the main purpose of the Greenock call was to rendezvous with three other ships of their new flotilla. The *Kipling, Kashmir* and *Jersey* joined the leader in the Clyde and together they covered the wide front of Western Approaches down to its Cornish salient. Land's End they rounded, in heavy weather, and steamed into the hunting grounds of the U-boats. On January 18th the four ships sailed into Plymouth Sound.

Destroyers cutting the blue sheen of the Sound are a grand sight from the Hoe. There Drake stands, watching his island and the grey ships that stand in from the bright horizon. One wonders if he winked his salty weather eye when the *Kelly* passed, and growled to the clouds above, 'What's she going to get up to now?' The day was tranquil when the flotilla sailed into the green arms of the harbour. Up in their holiday of air white seabirds danced.

And this was to be her home for several weeks to come. The Fifth were members now of the Western Approaches Striking Force. From now on, as long as they were at Plymouth, the *Kelly* was always under two hours' notice for steam. There were plenty of jobs to be done and they came thick and fast.

The next three months they spent almost entirely at sea. In that continuous bout of sea-time they must have spent longer on the French coast than on the English.

Three ships were giving us a great deal of trouble at this time: the eight-inch cruiser *Admiral Hipper* and the battle-cruisers *Scharnhorst* and *Gneisenau.* During the first three months of 1941 they were all out on our convoy routes, sinking our merchantmen. The *Hipper* sank her first ship on Christmas Day of the old year, and by March, when she returned to Germany for a refit, she had sunk seven more. Not a huge haul, but damaging enough. In the same period the two battle-cruisers sank or captured twenty-two merchant ships. If they had been forced to rely on home bases for rest and refreshment the three months' rampage of these ships would have been curtailed severely. But until the time came for a major refit they could forget about the Fatherland. Now they could range the wide Atlantic, smug in the knowledge that the long arm of Brittany stretched out towards them, with the port of Brest open-handed at its extremity. The *Hipper* came to Brest for the New Year before starting a second cruise, and returned there again at the end of February, after a profitable encounter with an unescorted convoy off the Azores, of which she had managed to sink seven ships before merciful fog shrouded the remaining twelve. The *Scharnhorst* and the *Gneisenau* had broken out from their home waters and made a dash into the Atlantic in early February. They finished their marauding cruise at the end of March and put into Brest. After that they remained on the French coast, penned in by the Royal Air Force, until they fled up the Channel a year later.

From Plymouth to Ushant is about one hundred and twenty miles, a mere few hours' steaming for the *Kelly* and her flotilla.

The *Hipper* was their *bête noire.* One day they received

a report that the German cruiser was making a break through the Channel. The four destroyers left Plymouth in a hurry and steamed flat out towards Dover. As soon as they left harbour they went to action stations and stayed there. Then Captain Mountbatten spoke to his Kellys over the loudspeaker. He began in his usual way.

'This is the Kelly Local News,' he announced. 'The *Hipper* has just left Brest and is making her way through the English Channel in company with twelve destroyers and an unknown number of E-boats. This is the plan. 'A' and 'B' mountings will engage the destroyers and 'X' mounting will concentrate on the E-boats. As they probably will not be able to see them they will have to fire at their sound, using H.A. projectiles. The torpedo crew will stand by to torpedo the *Hipper*. That is all.'

They heard this with some foreboding.

'We've got one chance,' said Taff to his oppo.

'What's that?' asked the other.

'That we don't catch up with the *Hipper*!'

In the end no one caught up with the *Hipper*. There were not enough ships to chase and trap her, as too many of our available ships were employed in other ways. The strength that might have been attacking the German raiders was defending the convoys. If we could not be certain of hunting out German warships on their own ground, at least we could meet them when they crossed the fence and ward off most of their blows at our merchant shipping. The warships left after that commitment had been met were too few and too busy for the Admiralty to be able to concentrate a sufficiently powerful striking force at any given point within its wide sphere of operations.

Late one evening, when the *Kelly* was going from Londonderry to Gibraltar to escort a damaged battleship home, she received a report that the *Scharnhorst* and the *Gneisenau* were making for the French Atlantic coast. The Fifth Flotilla was ordered to intercept. Mountbatten was standing in the chart-house with Butler-Bowdon and two or three other officers when the message was handed to him. Immediately he called up the bridge voice-pipe:

'Hard-a-port. Make the signal for thirty knots.'

The Admiralty message gave the course of the German battle-cruisers as heading for St Nazaire, but Mountbatten felt certain that the enemy was in fact making for Brest and asked Butler-Bowdon to lay him off a course for Brest. Then, when the *Kelly* had led around, he gave the Officer of the Watch the exact course to stay on. The rest of the flotilla already in line ahead, followed round. At that point the Captain addressed the ship's company over the loud-speaker system.

'The *Scharnhorst* and *Gneisenau*, together with the *Prinz Eugen*,' he told them, 'have got past our blockade and are now loose in the Atlantic. They have been spotted, however, and engaged by heavy units of the Home Fleet. Unfortunately, they have managed to slip away in very misty weather and as far as we know are heading for Brest. This is where we come in. Judging by their last-known course and speed they should be in the vicinity of Brest during the early morning. We are now going to lay in wait for them. We shall ignore any small fry we see, but on spotting the German battle-cruisers we shall carry out a torpedo attack.' He paused there for a second, then went on, 'Having sunk them, we shall then deal with the small fry.'

The flotilla steamed at full speed for Brest. Fast as they were, however, they were too late. No *Scharmhorst* or *Gneisenau* appeared.

During the cloudy days that followed this fruitless dash no air reconnaissance was possible and Mountbatten was severely criticised for ignoring the Admiralty message and making for Brest. On the first fine day, however, the R.A.F. spotted the battle-cruisers in Brest harbour. Mountbatten had been right but, unfortunately, about an hour and a half too late.

They still kept an eye on the *Hipper.* On one occasion they chased the heavy cruiser, or her ghost, as far north as the Faroes. It was immediately after that fruitless chase that history repeated itself once more. On their way south the *Kelly* called in at Londonderry, where they showed the flag in a special *Kelly* recruiting campaign. Three days later she cast off again and, putting her nose right into the teeth of some very nasty Irish weather, headed back towards her base. The weather deteriorated rapidly and the ship began to make very heavy going of it.

Taff was bridge messenger and was busy hanging on to the side of the chart-table, when the sub-lieutenant on watch sent him aft to fetch a towel and handkerchief from his cabin. Taff rolled his way along the sea side of the deck and dived into the wardroom flat just as a big sea showered the after tubes with white water. He got the articles and stuffed them inside his duffle-coat so as to have his hands free for gripping the lifeline on his return journey to the bridge. He came out of the after flat and turned round to put the clips on the door. He made the door fast and was just turning for'ard, when he saw a huge dark wave towering over the ship. He grabbed the rail running round the after flat and waited for the giant wave to hit him. There was a shattering roar. The whole ship disappeared and Taff was sucked off the rail and driven headlong through the sea. He hit the guardrail with a painful crash just as the ship started to roll back again. He picked himself up and staggered for'ard – to report to Subby that the wave had taken towel and handkerchief. 'And bloody nearly me with 'em,' said Taff under his breath.

He used to spend most of such watches on call in the signal distributing office just under the bridge. A little later that same night the ship was hit by another monster sea and did a terrible roll to starboard. For a few agonising seconds she hung there, while everyone on watch died a thousand deaths. Then, slowly, she righted herself.

'Third time lucky,' said old Tusky Hales, certain that his pet theory would even yet be vindicated and that she would turn over.

Taff was summoned to the bridge.

'Go and shake the shipwright and tell him to go and cut the whaler adrift,' was the order.

'Hello, what's happened now?' said Taff to himself as he doubled away. He went below, shook Chippy as ordered, then went on to the upper deck to see for himself. When he opened the fo'c'sle door he saw a scene of wrack and ruin. Once more in her short history the *Kelly* had lost her whaler, her motor-boat and all the guardrails on the starboard side, together with her Carley floats and all the abandon-ship gear. It wasn't fair.

Back in Plymouth, the ship had to spend some time refitting. While new guardrails, boats and other gear to replace that lost in the Irish Sea were being fitted, the opportunity was taken to install two of the new quick-firing Oerlikon anti-aircraft cannon.

The fitting of these guns aboard his own ship and the other vessels of the Fleet was a personal triumph for the *Kelly*'s Captain. Without his championship the gun would never have gone into service with the Navy. For several years before the war he had seen the great potentialities of the weapon and had fought for it at the Admiralty. Senior officers with more brass on their hats than brains in their heads had continued to dismiss the gun arbitrarily as 'fit for scrap iron'. However, war swept aside all such objections and the Oerlikon went into production.

If this gun had been adopted when its great merits had been first demonstrated the Fleet would have had an answer to the German dive-bombers and several fine ships might have been saved. The Oerlikon fired five hundred high explosive shells per minute and had a muzzle velocity almost twice that of any other gun of its weight.

Soon they were at sea again, hugging the French coast.

'I don't know why Jerry don't give us a mooring berth

over here,' said Rocky Wilkins, hunched up on the pom-pom platform, which slowly revolved in eccentric circles round the sky as the ship rolled.

One of their routine jobs was the escorting of minelayers who were placing their minefields along the enemy-occupied coast to bottle up the German Navy in its French harbours. The *Kelly* would often escort the new cruiser-minelayer *Abdiel* across to Brittany. Destroyers think they are fast, but when the job was finished the *Abdiel* would lower her stern and leave the 'ocean greyhound' standing. It was the *Kelly*'s job, on the minelaying expeditions, to 'take the place of honour', as the Captain called it, between the minelayers and the shore batteries and engage the latter if they opened fire. Shells from the shore batteries were not the only things they had to dodge, of course, and the ship's ack-ack armament was in constant action.

But, close as the minelaying squadron got to the coast, they could not rest, but continued to press in closer. One night they went particularly close into the approaches to the port, almost into the outer harbour of Brest itself.

A good many men had their hearts in their mouths that night. Taff admitted to himself that he was scared stiff but steeled himself by thinking of the Captain.

'If he's not afraid, why should I be?' he asked himself.

Dive-bombers found them with the early light, and they were bombed half the way back. But they survived.

One morning they returned to harbour about five o'clock to learn that the King would be visiting the ship during the forenoon. So they were set to work scrubbing and polishing and giving everything that extra shine. His Majesty arrived on board just after half-past ten, and after inspecting the ship's company said he was very impressed with what he had seen. In honour of the visit they were granted the first all-night leave they had had for a very long time.

The early part of the evening passed agreeably. But

later they wished they were back on the French coast. For that night Plymouth had her first blitz. Watch ashore agreed that they would have felt much safer in Brest harbour.

Ted West was watch aboard that night. When the sirens went he closed up at his action stations as C.O. of the transmitting station. The *Kelly,* in conjunction with neighbouring shore batteries, had her own sector for putting up a barrage, and it was not long before her 4.7s were blazing away. Down below in the T.S. West had no idea of what was happening ashore. After a lifetime of suspense there came a lull, and finally the all-clear.

Going on to the upper deck West was shocked to see what seemed to be the whole city on fire. Going ashore a few hours later he was even more shocked to discover that the whole of George Street, Princess Square, Bedford Street, and Guildhall, lovely St Andrew's Church and the upper end of Union Street had been burned and bombed to the ground. That was only the beginning for Plymouth, though the *Kelly* was not there to see the final assault on the town.

The flotilla continued to haunt the Channel area. Although they witnessed the savage attacks of the Luftwaffe on our towns, the men of the Fifth were heartened, on their trips to France, to see the R.A.F. taking the strap to the Nazis in return.

'We're between one burning coast and another,' said Taff, 'I don't know why each side doesn't start its own fires. It would save a lot of trouble.'

One winter's day when the ship was at Plymouth the starboard watch was returning from leave in bitter snowy weather. One leading stoker was leaving his home in the North of England to catch his train, when he slipped up on the frozen street and dislocated his ankle. Somehow, in spite of the pain, he struggled on and caught the train, managed to change trains in London and was helped down by his messmates to the ship. The Captain happened to be standing on the upper deck when the man hobbled aboard on the arm of his messmates. When he heard the full facts of the case he decided that some special award was called for. Shortly afterwards he cleared lower deck and said:

'You all know by now that any man breaking his leave and returning to the ship adrift is usually punished by having his leave stopped. In this case I intend to apply the reverse treatment. When a man manages to struggle back to the ship, in spite of the pain of a dislocated ankle, he deserves some kind of recognition. I think it is fitting that he should be given leave with both watches when leave is next piped.'

So routine went on its way, the routine of a destroyer in wartime, with more of the odd-job man in it than the 'ocean greyhound'.

Every Saturday was Captain's Rounds, when Lord Mountbatten would inspect the ship from stem to stern. War or no war, this routine is always strictly adhered to in the Navy. West was proud of his messdecks now. All his efforts, his bullying and his cajolery had achieved results. He felt with some pride that the *Kelly* had the cleanest and brightest messdecks in the whole flotilla. But that was as it should be, for the leader should set an example to the rest of the division.

On one particular Saturday forenoon West had spurred the cooks and sweepers on to make the after seamen's messdeck vie with the for'ard, and the stokers' with the signalmen's. Everything was sparkling, neat and shipshape, and West was waiting to stand rounds on the after messdeck. Looking around for last-minute improvements, he noticed something out of place on one of the mess shelves and told the cook to square it off. The cook had clumsy fingers and knocked a large open tin of pusser's peas to the deck just as West heard the quartermaster piping the Captain on his rounds. Peas were still rolling about the deck when Lord Mountbatten arrived. He even trod on one or two. West threw a black look at the wretched cook of the mess, but the Captain went for'ard with a grin on his face.

Another thing which amused the Captain was a quite remarkable collection of pin-ups pasted on the gun support of 'B' gun where is passed through the petty officers' mess. One Saturday afternoon, when the ship was lying in the dockyard at Portsmouth, the Captain came aboard over the fo'c'sle brow with Lady Mountbatten. He must have told his wife that the petty officers of the *Kelly* were keen students of art, because he lifted her up to gaze through the porthole at their pin-ups.

Life went by in a mixture of weary, often dangerous routine, and the never-failing gift of sailors for seeing the funny side of existence.

The atmosphere in the wardroom had remained very much the same. Most of the officers of the *Kelly*'s original ship's company were still with her, although the spice of life had been kept hot by a few changes.

The two chain pipe smokers, 'Torps' and his assistant, Sub-Lieutenant Turnbull, made sure of a constant supply of foul air. Goodenough was such an addict that he once tried to smoke his briar with a gas-mask on. He nearly suffocated and had to be revived by some hastily improvised artificial respiration. He was a man who never suffered fools gladly and was not above telling very senior officers where they got off. Signals he knew almost as well as his own job, and he used to infuriate Dunsterville, the Signals Officer, by calling out the correct flags direct to the Yeoman of Signals when the *Kelly* was carrying out a torpedo attack. In fact 'versatility' seemed to be his second name. As well as his various professional qualifications he was an expert clock repairer and a grower of prize roses.

'Dusty' Dunsterville himself was an amusing man with a quick wit. One morning he was climbing the bridge ladder, when the starboard lookout sang out:

'Mine bearing green four-O!'

Flags realised that it was one of our own mines which had come adrift. Looking at the seaman with a straight face he said:

'Mine is friendly.'

At once the lookout turned round and bawled:

'Mine is friendly, sir!'

Dunsterville's assistant was a warrant telegraphist. His real name was Pinder, but no one ever used it. He was a big man, so between one thing and another he became known as The Giant Panda.

Another sailor with a sense of humour was 'Winger' Pattison, the Secretary's assistant and a paymaster sub-lieutenant in the Royal Naval Reserve. Winger used to recite an unprintable poem called 'Mrs Bugle', which invariably brought the house down.

Commander Evans's quiet wit was highly appreciated. Once at dinner the Captain's secretary was grumbling about the flotilla staff, of which Commander Evans was one, and saying what a nuisance they all were.

'When I write my memoirs,' he growled, 'I shall call them "Toads I Have Known".'

'Oh no you won't, Scratch,' said Evans; 'you'll call them "Forever With The Lord".'

CHAPTER IX

THE CRUELLEST MONTH

MARCH, according to form, went out like a lamb, and the reason was not far to seek. The lion had moved to the Mediterranean.

The men of the *Kelly* could hear its roar from Plymouth. Ever since Christmas hot news had been coming in from the Med. The Kellys were particularly interested because the 'other half' of the 'J' and 'K' destroyers were operating from Malta under Captain Mack, who led his flotilla in the *Jervis,* the ship that had once lain alongside the *Kelly* in Hawthorn Leslie's yard, the ship that had once been 'No. 614' to the *Kelly*'s '615'.

Until Christmas 1940 Admiral Cunningham had had only the Italians to contend with, but after Taranto they were a beaten nation. The Italian Fleet moved its main base from Taranto to Naples, where the R.A.F. saw to it that they remained. The Wellingtons from Malta also bombed the battleships that still lay in dock in Taranto.

All over the Mediterranean our forces were hitting the Italians. Our submarines lurked in the shallow waters, and boats like the *Swordfish* and the *Truant* torpedoed and sank many thousands of tons of enemy shipping on its way either to Greece, where the Italians were falling back in disorder and disgrace, or to North Africa, where General Wavell drove them steadily back upon Libya. All units of the Fleet put constantly to sea to cover large convoys going to Greece or Malta, and the *Illustrious* sent her aircraft to strike the Dodecanese Islands.

Then the Navy brought the old year to a close with a flourish. Admiral Pridham-Wippell took his cruisers and destroyers on a sweep of the Adriatic, while the *Warspite* and the *Valiant* bombarded Valona, in Albania, where Italian troops and supplies were being marshalled for their wretched Greek war. After the bombardment the flagship called in at Malta before returning to Alexandria on Christmas Eve. It was Drake and the Spanish Main all over again – and all in Mussolini's 'Mare Nostrum'. The Greek navy popped a fire-cracker in the Duce's stocking, too. Their destroyers emulated the splendid Greek army and swept the Adriatic, while two of their submarines, *Papanikolis* and *Katsonis*, vied with our own *Swordfish* and *Truant* in sinking enemy troopships and tankers.

All this was cause for alarm in Berlin. After the Battle of Britain and the consequent postponement of Operation Sea Lion, Hitler had two major interdependent plans on the table.

Halted, for the moment, in the west, he did an about-face and began planning for his long awaited attack on Russia. Before she could feel confident of this attack Germany must have control of Rumania, both for her value as a jumping-off base against Russia and for her invaluable oil. The coercion of Rumania was no problem, but her protection from the Mediterranean side demanded that Turkey should be neutralised and the rest of the Balkans knocked out, particularly Greece, from which

British forces might strike north and British bombers raid the Rumanian oilfields. So the southern flank of the Russian front must be buttressed against attack, the 'soft underbelly' armoured against us. The Balkans must be occupied. German troops passed through Hungary and took over Rumania in October. The drive through the Balkans had begun.

But the Balkan offensive was also part of another plan. The German army, which was preparing, towards the end of 1940, to conquer Yugoslavia and Greece, formed the left claw of a giant pincer movement aimed at the Middle East, of which the Italian army in Libya was the right claw. By a concerted drive through the Balkan peninsula and through Egypt the heart of British resistance in the Mediterranean was to be broken. After that the road would lie open to the East, where Japan was even now looking for the right time and place to begin her own road to conquest.

That was the theory – two birds with one stone. But there was a big flaw in the plan, a flaw which in time was to help bring it to ruin. Hitler needed a successful Italy for its execution, and by the end of 1940 he had given up all hope of that. First, Mussolini had been disgraced in Greece, and Greek troops had even invaded Albania. But this was less serious than the shameful debacle in North Africa, where the British Army of the Nile was thrashing an Italian army many times its size – the army that was to have been the strong right arm of the Axis against the Middle East. He saw that he would have to take strong measures to save the business and make good the damage already done by his inept partner. He acted swiftly.

On January 10th the *Illustrious*, escorting a convoy through to Malta and Greece, suddenly found herself under overwhelming attack by Stukas and Junkers 88s. Concentrated dive-bombing seriously damaged the carrier, which only just managed to make Malta, where she drew all the fury of the bombers for a terrible fortnight, before she managed to slip away to Alexandria and out through Suez to the United States for repairs.

The Stukas came from Sicily, where Hitler had sent a heavy force of aircraft as the first step towards breaking British power in the Mediterranean. Their targets would be the ships of the Fleet and, in particular, its vital advanced base, Malta. They had already crippled the *Illustrious,* sunk the cruiser *Southampton* and began a cruel and devastating blitz upon tiny Malta. It was going to be the same old story – air power, with all the strength on one side. Following this first show of strength, Hitler planned a campaign against Greece and Crete for the spring and the landing of a German army in North Africa to drive Wavell back and capture Egypt. This time he meant to make the pincers work.

A poet said that 'April is the cruellest month'. April 1941 was certainly a cruel month for our forces in the Mediterranean, now the fight for the big prize of the Middle East was really on.

Round one, however, had gone to us. On March 28th Admiral Cunningham routed the Italian Fleet in a glorious victory at Matapan, and rammed the already meaningless words 'Mare Nostrum' right down the Duce's fat throat. But it was not enough to knock out the sleeping partner, for only three days after Matapan General Rommel, commanding the new German army in Africa, began his drive on the Nile.

The right pincer had struck first. The British army of the Nile fell back step by step before it. By now it was an enfeebled and reduced army, for the left pincer was about to strike, in the shape of the German thrust down through Greece and the Balkans, and the larger part of Wavell's army had been withdrawn from Africa and sent to Greece to meet it. The attack on Greece began on April 6th, a week after Rommel's successful push, and, from the start, promised to be every bit as successful. The British army there, too, was forced back, faced by enormously superior weight and with next to no air support. In fact it seemed that nothing could keep those pincers apart except the Navy.

In Greece the situation was declared hopeless on April 16th, when the decision was taken to evacuate all British troops and fall back upon Crete. The date for evacuation from Greece was set for the 28th, then hastily changed to the 24th, as the German advance gathered momentum. There were fifty thousand men in Greece, and the Navy had to get them off, with a skeleton fleet, under a sky dark with Nazi bombers.

They did it – at a price. Part of the price was paid in destroyers – the *Diamond* and the *Wryneck* sunk by dive-bombers while escorting the troopship *Slamat*, which was also sunk. Many other ships were also hit and badly damaged. On April 26th Athens Radio sent a last signal to Malta and Alexandria:

'Last night with you – happy days with victory and liberty – God with you and for you. Good luck.'

To this battered Malta replied:

'Very grateful for your message. The Medes and the Persians could not make it. How shall the modern Attila?'

And Alexandria, where the Fleet prepared itself for the battle to come, made a promise and a prophecy:

'We shall not forget you, and look forward to the day of freedom.'

Then silence and the darkness of defeat closed down on Greece. In that darkness the searchlight of action swung round and focused upon the island of Crete.

Meanwhile, in the comparatively peaceful waters of the Western Mediterranean, somewhere between Gibraltar and Malta, another naval force was steaming – the cruiser *Dido*, the minelayer *Abdiel*, *Kelly*'s old consort, and, not least, *Kelly* herself, leading the Fifth Flotilla.

It was not until *Kelly* cleared the Eddystone that Captain Mountbatten made an announcement and hinted that they were following the sun.

However, there had been warnings in recent weeks of a break in the old pattern. The war news definitely told them that the Mediterranean Fleet was badly in need of reinforcements. Then, just a few days before, they had embarked a detachment of Commandos for sea training. Some of the men had thought that this was the signal to move on.

Those soldiers were very bad sailors. They lay along the upper deck in dumb misery most of the trip. Ted West was amazed to see one of his messdeck sweepers, who normally succumbed to seasickness himself, swaggering around the upper deck in duffle-coat and seaboots, slapping the wretched Commandos on the back and telling them they would soon get used to it. West made a mental note of this sudden miraculous healing of the sick, intending to take it up with the man when he was next 'seasick'. The Commandos were very well equipped, and every man wore a superb leather jerkin. After twenty-four hours' 'sea training' they were disembarked, and West was at a loss to understand how a number of the *Kelly*'s ship's company happened to be wearing leather jerkins when they next left harbour.

On that trip the *Kelly*, as usual, shipped a lot of water, which spoiled an issue of cabbage stowed in the galley flat. The action of the salt water on the cabbage made it necessary to get rid of it quickly, as the smell was by no means exotic. West looked round for his messdeck sweeper, the man responsible for the galley flat, and found him once more stretched out with seasickness. West thought this strange after his behaviour with the Commandos and put him to work baling out the water in the galley flat, with the smell of the cabbage to keep him company. He did not need to sham seasickness for very long.

A few days after this they were sent, watch by watch, on three days' boiler-cleaning leave. It was then that they started putting two and two together. On their return they were issued with tropical kit and the ship began to take on board box after box of ack-ack shells, fifty-gallon drums of aviation spirit and crates of spare parts for fighter aircraft. To those who had been following the news from the Mediterranean this cargo was very significant. Finally they embarked another party of soldiers and put to sea.

They were not left long in doubt as to their general destination. Their first evening in Gibraltar was a revelation, after dreary, blacked-out England. The Rock blazed with light and the sight did them all a world of good. Somewhere in the gloom of war the soft lights of normality and peace still shone.

At Gibraltar they disembarked fifty very seasick soldiers, all very glad to get firm ground under their feet and profoundly thankful that they had not joined the Navy. The soldiers had brought a miscellaneous collection of equipment with them. On the first evening at sea the Officer of the Watch looked down aft from the bridge and said:

'Good God! That's the first time I've seen someone crossing the Bay on a motorbike.'

They left Gib and steered a westerly course. This raised many hopes that they might be proceeding to the Eastern Mediterranean by the Cape route, but as soon as darkness fell they turned about and headed for Malta.

The passage through the Straits to Malta had been completely closed to all British shipping since the Luftwaffe had come to the Mediterranean, crippling the *Illustrious* and sinking so many ships, and the Fifth Flotilla and its companions were the first unit to reopen the passage from west to east.

On their way the old hands were full of the delights of Malta.

'The island of bells and smells,' said one killick.

West had been telling the men what they could expect in the way of relaxation when they reached the island. There was plenty to do there, he told them: swimming, booze and the rest. No visit to that sun-kissed island, he said in true guidebook fashion, was complete without a visit to The Gut. The Gut, or Strait Street as it was more properly called, is a narrow, sloping alley of steps lined throughout its entire length with garish dance-halls, cafés and bars. The owners of these doubtful establishments vied with each other to lure the matelots inside.

'You'll go down there,' said West, 'and all the way they'll pop out and pull at your arm and say "Come inside, Jack. All your ship's company inside. They both drunk".'

He told them all about the charms of the Lucky Wheel and the Egyptian Queen, and reeled off a long string of bars in Valetta and Sliema where Jose dispensed ambit, the lethal local poison, to Jack Ashore.

When the news came through that the Fifth Flotilla was coming in the whole population of Valetta streamed out on to the battlements overlooking the harbour and gave them a rousing welcome.

As soon as they got through into Grand Harbour Ted West realised that this was a different Malta to the one he had known in the peaceful pre-war days. The *Kelly* berthed in the same position the *Illustrious* had occupied a few weeks before, when the Stukas had made her their main target and reduced the old Three Cities district around her to rubble. The people of the three ancient medieval 'cities' of Vitoriosa, Cispicua and Senglea now lived like primitive people in the caves cut in the rock beside the dockyard. When the *Kelly*'s wires went ashore the smoke and dust had not settled from the last raid, and before the last fender had been secured the alert went again.

'What are they all running for?' asked an O.D. scornfully.

He soon found out. The Nazi airmen were pleased to see the empty berth occupied again and a few near misses soon drove everyone down below. Mountbatten gave orders that throughout the flotilla at least half the ship's company should take cover in the shelters on the alert, leaving the other half to provide guns' crews and fire parties. This order included the captains and first lieutenants, but unfortunately there was no one to give the order to Captain (D) himself, so Mountbatten used to remain aboard.

They watched in amazement the fury of the Nazi blitz on the island, so much worse than anything they had seen before. Dive-bombers made the bright days one long, unending nightmare with their screaming savagery, though the few Royal Air Force Hurricanes and Spitfires could be seen diving down through the shells of their own barrage to catch the Stukas.

'Piece of cake just after they've pulled out,' said one young pilot officer ashore. 'Just push 'em into the drink.'

But our fighter pilots were taking on almost impossible odds, with no guarantee of reinforcements themselves. One day the men on the *Kelly*'s guns watched a Hurricane catch fire above Grand Harbour and fall in flames straight on to a little bar called The First and Last that was very popular with them. It seemed to them as if the whole hatred of Germany was being hurled at Malta. No one got any rest there, from the A.O.C. to the 'erk' filling in bomb craters on Luqa, Takali or Hal Far airfields so that bombers and naval torpedo planes could take off and attack Rommel's convoys, and the handful of fighters could get into the shell-shocked air to defend their precious base. You felt you hardly had time to take breath between raids.

If they went ashore it was usually a question of one quick noggin and a dash for shelter. At first they found that Jose would rush to the shelters at the first sound of the warning, leaving all his bottles of booze in the bar. After a short while, however, he got wise and would keep only one or two bottles in the bar, which he could snatch up, together with his money-bag, as soon as it was time to take cover.

They heard all about the early days of the war in

Malta, when Mussolini had sent his eagles over Malta to bomb the little island, which was such a thorn in his obese flesh, and snatch a quick and easy victory. Malta then had been defended by a hastily assembled scratch flight of three obsolete Sea-Gladiator aircraft nicknamed 'Faith, Hope and Charity', and flown by Royal Air Force pilots, most of them from flying-boats, who had volunteered to fly the old aircraft against the modern Italian fighters and bombers. They performed their duties so well that they shot down a large number of enemy planes and forced the Italians to abandon all hope of an easy victory over Malta. They hung on for two grim months, flying from bomb-torn airstrips, fighting superior numbers, continual bombing and fatigue, until only one of their precious Gladiators was left, the aircraft called 'Faith'. It was only then that a few Hurricanes had arrived to take over the defence.

The names of these pilots were still on everyone's lips – Peter Keeble, who had been killed; Peter Hartley, badly burned when his aircraft caught fire over Grand Harbour; Jock Martin, the C.O. of Fighter Flight, who used to prop a sunshade over the cockpit and read a book while waiting on the airstrip at Hal Far for the order to scramble; and George Burges, the A.O.C.'s personal pilot, who was the 'ace' of the little squadron and whose picture, cut from *The Times of Malta*, still adorned many a little shrine in the yellow rock caves and the ancient catacombs beneath Valetta, where the Maltese sheltered from the battle ranging above and prayed for the pilots defending them.

The *Kelly*'s main job was to carry out nightly sweeps to prevent the flow of supplies from reaching Rommel's army in Africa. The mere fact that a flotilla was known to be patrolling the supply lines prevented the enemy convoys from sailing.

The flotilla had a regular drill for these occasions. As evening approached the destroyers raised steam automatically for full speed, ready to leave harbour by seven o'clock. Before this, Captain Mountbatten and the Flotilla Navigator, Butler-Bowden, used to go up to the Headquarters at Lescaris to await the result of the air reconnaissance of the convoy routes and according to these results to receive the Admiral's instructions on whether the flotilla was to proceed to sea to intercept the shipping or remain in harbour.

The ship's company soon found that they could get more sleep at sea than in harbour, as the bombing was at all times vicious and prolonged. Entertainment ashore was non-existent. All the bright lights and laughter had gone from Malta. The Gut was deserted and nearly all its cafés and bars closed – the Lucky Wheel, the Egyptian Queen and the rest. The sunlit streets, normally alive with people, were blocked with fallen debris and filled with smoke and choking yellow dust. Catastrophe had struck the island, and the loyalty of the Maltese was costing them dear.

But there were occasional lulls, when the Kellys went ashore and loafed in the sunshine. They even managed to get an occasional game of football. Sometimes there was leisure to bask in those warm nights of the early Mediterranean spring, to hold free and easy sing-songs, to bathe in the creeks and harbours around the coast.

Once, between raids, the ship's company were having their photograph taken by a Maltese and his young assistant. Suddenly the sirens wailed and the two photographers took to their heels in opposite directions, only to bounce off the guardails on either side of the ship. When the all-clear was sounded they were persuaded to try again. Once more the sirens went. This time they both cleared the guardrails like Olympic hurdlers and went overboard, to be picked up by dghaisas from the harbour. It was some days before they got another chance, but eventually a lull in the bombing enabled the Kellys to smile and say 'cheese' long enough to have their likenesses recorded for what was then a doubtful posterity.

One of their operations from Malta was a bombardment of Benghazi, in support of our hard-pressed army. The town had been in Axis hands about a month and was being used to supply Rommel's army. Any damage that could be done to shipping in the harbour and to dock installations would greatly relieve the pressure on the Army of the Nile.

The night of the shoot was brilliant with moonlight. Everything had been prepared. Each destroyer was to fire two hundred rounds of 4.7 high explosive, while the four-inch high-angle guns were to fire starshell to illuminate the target.

Swiftly they approached the dark line of the shore. The old lighthouse on the hill could be clearly seen, silhouetted against the moonlit sky. They steamed on towards the harbour, having split up into two units about a mile apart.

The guns of both units were ready to open fire simultaneously by signal when a certain position had been reached. It soon became clear to the Flotilla Navigator that the force would make its landfall about half a mile too far to the north and that accordingly the *Kelly* and her consorts would be unable to fire through the breakwater entrance, which was the only way of damaging the ships sheltering alongside in the harbour. As it appeared that the flotilla had not yet been discovered by the enemy, the Captain decided to make a short leg to seaward. As soon as the flotilla was re-formed on the correct line of bearing they turned in again at twelve knots. When the exact position was reached, all guns opened fire on the shipping inside the harbour, now clearly seen against the light. Just as the order to cease fire was given the first gun opened up ashore. The flotilla left harbour at thirty knots, making smoke to cover their retreat, leaving a smashed chaos of burning, sinking wrecks behind them. At sea they were bombed, but they zigzagged and dropped smoke floats and eventually threw off their attackers.

They had paralysed the shipping in Benghazi harbour, but their luck was out when it came to catching ships at sea. The Italians had been severely shaken by now and behaved very warily towards the new striking force. Captain Mountbatten nearly broke the ship up several times trying to catch the elusive Eyeties. One chase in heavy weather cost them yet another whaler, another motor-boat and the guardrails that had been fitted after their monumental roll in the Irish Sea. This was their third set.

'Very 'eavy on boats, is this tub,' said one old torpedo-man sadly.

Down below everyone went down on their hands and knees and ate their meals off the deck. It was useless trying to keep food on the table. The deck was permanently slippery with squashed pusser's peas.

So, between dodging the bombs in Malta and patrolling the dangerous waters between there and the African coast, the *Kelly* and the Fifth found time going rapidly by.

They had soon got a name for themselves in their new sphere of operations. Once upon a time, it is told, the quartermaster on watch aboard the *Warspite* was heard to pipe:

'The ship now passing to starboard is Lord Louis Mountbatten and his gang of pirates.'

Going into Grand Harbour one day the third ship in the line, the *Jersey,* struck a mine in the entrance and sank, completely blocking the fairway. After survivors had been taken off, with very prompt assistance of the dghaisa men in the harbour, Captain Mountbatten set about clearing the channel. A passage had to be buoyed in the fairway so that they could get out. The Torpedo Officer with one signalman took one jetty, and the Navigating Officer and two signalmen took the other, on the opposite side of the harbour. For nine hours that day, and six hours the next, they roasted in the hot sun on the harbour walls. The signalmen, acting on instructions from the officers, guided the cutter which was rowing backwards and forwards dropping dan buoys to mark the clear channel. Captain Mountbatten sent the *Jersey* survivors home by the next available transport.

The flotilla was bottled up again on another occasion when the Germans sowed magnetic mines in the entrance to Grand Harbour. This time they were left cooling their heels a little longer. All the minesweepers based on Malta had been sunk by the bombers, but eventually, acting on instructions received from the Fleet Torpedo Officer in Alexandria, they cleared the obstructions by blowing them up with depth-charges.

One afternoon, after a particularly heavy raid, Gordon Rogers went up to his favourite sun-bathing spot on the front of 'A' gun between the twin barrels. When he got there this time he found the place occupied. With feathers ruffled and eyes tightly closed, a tiny green bird was strutting dazedly round on the hot metal.

He offered no resistance and made no attempt to fly away when the stoker picked him up gently and carried him below to the mess.

'It's a budgerigar, Rog,' said someone. 'See if you can make him talk.'

But Joey was not in voice – the bombs had stunned him into silence. Presently Gordon went to work and made him a cage. There the budgerigar recovered somewhat from his shell-shock.

As soon as he had decided to keep the bird Rogers put in for official permission to do so. He scribbled his request on an old bit of a cigarette packet and gave it to the Chief Stoker. Chiefie re-wrote and re-worded it, making the request, as he thought, quite clear, and in due course Gordon came up before the Captain.

'I see here that you wish to keep a canary aboard,' said Mountbatten.

'Er, yes, sir,' said Rogers.

'Have you got it with you?' asked the Captain.

'Yes, sir, it's right here,' said the stoker, and lifted up Joey in his cage for inspection.

Mountbatten looked closely at the bird.

'That's not a canary,' he said; 'that's a budgerigar. Why is it down here as a canary?'

'I don't know, sir,' said Rogers.

'Perhaps the Chief Stoker couldn't spell "budgerigar",' said Mountbatten with a grin.

Rogers was allowed to keep the bird, and Joey went on living on the stokers' messdeck.

But they could never persuade him to sing, or even say his name. Perhaps it was the terror of the blitz.

Perhaps he knew what was coming.

On May 21st, when the *Kelly* had been operating from Malta for three hectic weeks, Lord Mountbatten cleared lower deck and told the ship's company that the enemy were attacking Crete in great force. It was the Navy's job, he told them, to prevent the Germans from making a seaborne landing on the island. For that vital job every ship would be needed, so the Fifth Flotilla were to go to Cretan waters to assist their already hard-pressed colleagues in fighting off the Nazis.

The German invasion of Crete had begun the day before. Under cover of heavy bombing and machine-gunning attacks convoys of troop-carrying gliders, escorted by fighters and supported by dive-bombers, began coming in, followed by waves of parachute troops. The parachutists and the rest were the army's pidgin. The Navy kept its eyes to sea-ward. The main Fleet took up position west of Crete in case the Italian Fleet should try to intervene, while Rear-Admirals Glennie and King patrolled with their forces of cruisers and destroyers in the Aegean.

The Navy's ordeal began at daylight on the 21st. From then on all units were bombed incessantly. At one o'clock came the first casualty, the destroyer *Juno*, sunk by bombs in sixty seconds. The cruiser *Ajax* was damaged in the forenoon, but got her revenge half an hour before midnight when Admiral Glennie, with the cruisers *Dido, Orion* and *Ajax*, and the destroyers *Kimberley, Hasty, Hereward* and *Janus,* annihilated a German convoy carrying four thousand soldiers to Crete. Early next morning Admiral King's squadron, the cruisers *Calcutta, Perth, Naiad* and *Carlisle,* with the destroyers *Kandahar, Kingston* and *Nubian,* attacked another convoy, leaving most of its ships sinking or on fire. By that time ammunition, particularly for the anti-aircraft guns, was running low and air attacks were increasing to a furious pitch. When Admiral King had sunk everything within the range of his guns, he called off his destroyers, which were pursuing the surviving units of the enemy force into their covering smoke screen, and steered westward towards the main Fleet.

All that morning they were bombed continually. Waves of Stukas came in against them out of the sun. The *Naiad* was damaged and some of her compartments flooded after she had sustained thirty-six near misses. Then the *Carlisle* was hit and set on fire and her Captain killed. The *Kingston* immediately came alongside her to give assistance, but was received by the signal: 'Keep clear of me.' The *Carlisle* put out her fires and continued to put up a furious barrage against the enemy. Shortly after one o'clock the *Naiad* dodged a torpedo attack, just as the Battle Fleet was sighted to the west. The battleships then came under attack and both the *Warspite* and the *Valiant* were hit. By now the destroyers had suffered another loss. The *Greyhound* had been sunk by eight dive-bombers. The *Kandahar* and the *Kingston* went to rescue her crew, supported by the cruisers *Fiji* and *Gloucester*. The *Gloucester* was hit again and again and set on fire, until she finally stopped in a sinking condition. The Germans came down and machine-gunned the survivors in the water. The remainder of the force withdrew under continual bombing. At seven o'clock two bombs hit the *Fiji* and she sank.

The Battle Fleet, cruising in Kithera Channel, was the steady rock upon which all units relied and on which they closed for the greater protection of weight and numbers at the climax of the air blitz. In the afternoon the *Kelly, Kashmir, Kipling, Kelvin* and *Jackal* joined the Fleet.

The first hours of their dash from Malta had been peaceful, unbelievably tranquil and calm as the ships steamed through the blue and gold beauty of a Mediterranean morning.

Down below on the *Kelly*'s messdeck a very new able seaman was singing:

> Oh my darlin' Maggie May, they 'ave taken you away,
> And I'll never see my darlin' any more.
> She betrayed all the sailors and the captains of the whalers
> The first time that they put in from sea.

His killick looked at him in disgust.

'Listen to Jack-my-Hearty,' he said. 'Blimey, no-badge A.B.'s! I've spit 'em!'

'Well, spit us a couple more then an' we'll 'ave a crafty 'and of solo,' said the sprog, digging deep into his new repertoire of slang. 'Ere, 'ooks, where we 'eadin' for?' he asked.

'Crete,' said the killick morosely.

'Oh,' said the no-badgeman, none the wiser. 'What's Crete like then, mate?'

'Crete? Dirty big sunbaked rock in the middle of the 'ogwash,' came the sour reply. 'Olive groves, vines and that sort of thing. I was there once before the war.' His face softened. 'Very beautiful it all was, really. Oranges, I remember, big and bright, glowin' on the green; used to make it look as if the blinkin' tree was on fire. And little green lanterns they used to put in the cemeteries, on the graves at night – used to shine in the dark like fireflies.' He paused, his eyes bright as he remembered. He chuckled.

'I remember going to one house and they gave us a glass of water and a little dish of jam.'

'Is that all they 'ad?' asked Young England.

'No, stupid; that's one of their customs,' said the killick. He paused again and reflected. 'Very old is Crete. They had a civilisation there thousands of years ago – a real civilisation, not the excuse for a madhouse we've got, a millennium – a thousand years of peace and plenty.'

'Cor!' said the sprog, his mouth open. All this was as the sound of flutes to him.

And, like the echo of an antique Pan-pipe, the thought of peace curled up into the sunlight, driven by unspoken longings into the lazy heat, like an innocent fawn's dream, floating, drifting . . . until it was broken by the clang of alarm bells and the clatter of feet on steel ladders. Action stations.

It was a submarine. Asleep, apparently, drowsed or drunken in the heat of noon, she lay torpid, like a basking shark, and did not wake until the *Kelly* was almost on her. Then she leapt up and crash-dived.

The destroyers immediately got a perfect ping. They riddled the sea around the contact with depth charges. Captain (D) wanted to stay and search for signs of a kill, but was ordered to proceed at once and join the Fleet. The submarine must almost certainly have been sunk. They steamed on, wondering what was in store for them in the hell of Crete.

The rating up in the range-finder was the first to sight anything. He had heard that the Eyetie Fleet was out, and the Captain had told them in his usual way that if enemy units were sighted it was their duty to attack them. Consequently, when he sighted those masts on the horizon he was a bit uneasy. He called up the bridge.

'Range-finder bridge. Ships bearing green 05,' he reported.

'Thank you,' returned the bridge.

Then:

'Range-finder bridge. Range 205.'

'Thank you, range-finder,' answered the bridge again; then, detecting the note of anxiety in the man's voice: 'It's all right, they're ours.'

It was the Battle Fleet, under heavy attack. They saw one Stuka come right down through the fire and score a hit on the *Warspite*. When they closed the flagship, the Admiral ordered them to go and pick up survivors from the *Gloucester* and the *Fiji*. The *Kelly* was uncertain of the position of the two sinkings and made the signal to the *Kingston:*

> Operating signal. Transmit your call sign on 270 kilocycles so that a D.F. bearing may be obtained.

When they reached the positions of the sunken ships, however, all the remaining survivors had been picked up.

Meanwhile, other signals were in the air. The Commander-in-Chief received an urgent message from the G.O.C. Crete.

> Naval bombardment of Maleme aerodrome would be appreciated.
>
> Time of origin 1856.

The Commander-in-Chief immediately signalled Captain (D) 5:

> Comply with G.O.C.'s signal 1856.

The *Kelly* then made to the *Kelvin* and *Jackal*, both of which had been detached for separate duty:

Am carrying out bombardment myself now.

Then there were three.

Before they had reached the north-west tip of Crete the *Kipling* was forced to drop out with defective steering gear.

Then there were two.

Darkness fell quickly, at it does in the Mediterranean, with no twilight to soften the transition from harsh daylight, and they made for Maleme. Their mission was urgent. German airborne troops had established themselves on this, one of Crete's only two airfields, and had thus opened the door to heavy airborne reinforcements. As they approached the airfield in the darkness everyone waited tensely, wondering what they would find.

The *Kelly's* radar was closed up all the time, and in the early hours the operator suddenly reported:

Echo bearing Red 80, range 030.

The echo turned out to be two caques, acting as troop transports, on their way to Maleme to reinforce the troops there.

It was a dead-still night, with no wind, and when the order 'Open shutters' rang out and the *Kelly*'s and the *Kashmir*'s searchlights splashed the troopships with light, the Germans were just lowering the sails. Both ships were jammed tight with soldiers, all heavily armed and with full packs on their backs. The destroyers let fly with all guns and the Nazis started jumping overboard in full equipment, shouting and screaming, and a few of them making the Nazi salute, yelling 'Heil Hitler' into the night. Having sunk both ships the *Kelly* picked up another troop-carrier. This one must have been loaded down to the gunwales with aviation spirit. She went up with a bang and burned like a Roman candle.

Then the two destroyers proceeded to carry out their

bombardment. They went in very close, to between one thousand and two thousand yards, and hit the airfield many times. Instead of their expected reinforcements, the German forces ashore got British shells. Although Maleme was in enemy hands, someone had placed lights at each side of the airfield on the water's edge to assist the bombarding ships.

By the time they had finished it had started getting light. Mountbatten knew that the Germans on Maleme must have radioed the position of the two British destroyers to their bombers, and he knew that they could expect trouble when dawn came.

Then, as soon as it got light, he received the signal:

> To Flag Officer 7th Cruiser Squadron, 5th Destroyer Flotilla, 14th Destroyer Flotilla. Ships addressed are to withdraw forthwith towards Alexandria.

The Fleet had now done all it could to save Crete. They had smashed the enemy's attempt at invasion by sea and, short of growing wings to provide our non-existent air support, their effort was spent. Ammunition was now getting very low, and the Commander-in-Chief had decided on a general withdrawal to Alexandria to refuel and re-arm.

The *Kelly* and the *Kashmir* immediately turned and headed south. As they steamed down the coast of Crete they were spotted by a single aircraft.

The dawn broke as only a dawn in the Mediterranean can – calm, bright and peaceful after the carnage of the night before.

On the pom-pom they could not remember how long they had been closed up at the gun. The gun captain looked at his crew, dirty, eyes red-rimmed, unshaven and desperately tired, and thought. 'Blimey, do I look like that, too?'

Then high-level bombers appeared. They showered

anti-personnel bombs all round the two ships, but there were no casualties and no one was unduly worried.

Rocky Wilkins turned to a young oppo of his.

'Here's a tanner, Wings,' he said. 'Go and get us a bar of nutty.'

Chief Petty Officer Primrose went to the Signals Officer and said:

'Sir, my lads are all in. Can't we pack up on two frequencies? – they've been up all night.'

He had just got the words out, when there was a report.

Radar bridge, radar bridge. Large formation of aircraft approaching from astern.

Stewart, in the range-finder, felt a tap on his shoulder. It was his trainer. He said:

'Look astern, look astern!'

Stewart looked.

'My God!' he said. He saw a black swarm of bombers coming in very low. Immediately he started pressing the cat-push, sending ranges down to the T.S. But they were all surface ranges and useless to the fire-control system.

Then the bombers were on them. All guns opened fire, West with his Oerlikon, Rocky Wilkins and the rest on the pom-pom, Lofty Howarth at his 4.7. They all blazed away as the Junkers roared over the masthead and dropped their bombs.

Primrose heard them peeling off and went down from the bridge to the cross-passage. There he heard a distant explosion. He bumped into Tusky Hales.

'The *Kashmir*'s gone,' said the G.I.

Just as he opened the door of the wireless office Primrose heard a loud explosion and felt the ship shudder beneath him.

Down aft on the four-inch, Beresford was shouting:

'Train this gun round!'

One man grabbed a broom and started knocking away

the empty cylinders that were blocking the swivel. He looked up and saw it falling from the plane – the bomb that hit them just abaft the engine-room as the *Kelly* was slewing round at thirty knots.

Almost immediately the ship started to turn over.

On the guns they hung on to cocking-levers, loading trays, anything they could get a grip on, as the ship heeled, still making speed, with the water rushing in through a great hole in her side.

Taff Davies, with most of his clothes blown off and his skin hanging from his body in strips, was leading a file of burnt and blackened scarecrows. The man immediately behind him was burned from head to foot and his ears had been burned off.

No one had left their posts, and all the guns were still firing.

Ted West got a Stuka square in his sights. A third of the way through its dive he opened fire and saw his tracers going right home and pieces breaking off the bomber, which burst into bright flame and crashed into the sea. After that things happened fast. Out of the corner of his eye he saw a parachute floating down, huge geysers of boiling spray spouting into the air from near misses and away on the port beam the *Kashmir,* a smoking wreck, broken in two and sinking. Gunfire and screaming bombers made a hell of the air. Then he saw a great column of flame shoot up from the after 4.7s. Mountbatten shouted:

'Keep all the guns firing – we've been hit!'

West got a stoppage in the Oerlikon. Quickly he unstrapped himself, cleared the gun and went on firing without strapping himself in again. This saved his life. The next moment the sea came up and hit him.

All over the ship the rising sea was washing them away from the guns. Lofty Howarth found himself trapped inside the gun shield, with the water rising over him.

The ship was over on her side now. One man, a telegraphist, had managed to struggle along the starboard passage to the for'ard boiler-room hatch. He made a wild jump for the doorway leading to the upper deck, missed it and fell back against the hatch. He tried to get free, but his leg was caught. There is a time at the crisis of a fever when the forces for and against life battle for a man's body. So it was now with him. He was almost giving up, when he thought of the one person that made the last supreme effort worth while. He thought in a flash, 'I've let you down, darling; I'll never get out of this.' Then he made one last, desperate leap and grabbed the door. The *Kelly* was over on her back now, but he saw a green patch of water under the great shadow of the ship above him. Gasping and choking, he kicked out towards the world of light.

Now they were all fighting for life in the dim light below the surface, all those who had been washed off the *Kelly*'s decks. Slowly they struggled against the suction of the ship, fighting the drag of the water, with the surface of the sea above them getting darker and the sun a deeper and deeper red. A man would hold his breath down there until his lungs seemed about to burst. There was singing in his ears, a daze of blood before his eyes. He thought of his wife, mother, father, the peaceful streets of his home town. He prayed, wildly. Then camly, he thought, 'So this is what it's like to drown.' Suddenly he was floating on the surface of the sea, with the sun shining in his eyes.

But they were the lucky ones. Down below many men were hopelessly trapped at their posts.

When the Stukas were sighted astern Commander Evans went below to the engine-room. There he found the Chief E.R.A. on the floorplates and said to him:

'Stand by for squalls; there's a host of aircraft coming up astern.'

Rogers had the morning watch on the engine-room throttles. With him, besides Commander Evans and the

Chief E.R.A., were another E.R.A. and a leading stoker, while the Chief Engineer's messenger, a 'Scouse' and a townie of Rogers', had stationed himself above the engine-room hatch. He was thus ideally placed to deliver a running commentary on what followed.

'Hey, Rog,' he shouted, poking his head down through the hatch, 'we're in for it now; there's about twenty-five of 'em coming up.'

The killick offered a word of advice.

'Go and get a cricket bat and bash off the bombs, then,' he yelled.

Above the roar of the engines they could hear the thunder of the bombers approaching, the screams of their engines as they peeled off for the attack and the racket from the *Kelly*'s guns.

Scouse yelled down through the hatch:

'They've got the *Kashmir,* she's sinking.'

'God help them,' thought Rogers. Just then there was a tremendous, dull jarring thud and the whole ship shook beneath them.

'Near miss,' said Commander Evans.

'I hope,' said the Chief E.R.9.

Th 'near miss' had put out all the lights and thrown Rogers flat on his back. In the dim glow of the secondary lighting Commander Evans looked at each man's face in turn, scrutinising them keenly for any signs of panic. What he saw satisfied him and he moved across to answer the bridge telephone which had suddenly started ringing. He took the receiver off but could only make out a confused babble of sound. There was certainly nobody speaking on the phone, so he replaced it. It rang again. Once again there was nothing on it but a confused noise. As he put it back on its hook the ship suddenly gave a lurch and started heeling over violently to port.

Evans fell against the phone and started to slide across the steeply canting floorplates. It was obvious now that the ship was capsizing.

'Get up, everybody!' he shouted, and they all started to climb. He himself had slid past the nearest ladder, but he began to climb up, using feed pumps, pipes, valves and anything he could get a purchase on. As the ship heeled over spanners and tools of all kinds came crashing down about their heads. Rogers ducked into the cover of an oil-fuel line. Below, he could see green water pouring in through the port and starboard hatches. The secondary lighting caught fire as the oil spilled out of the upturned lamps, then died away as the oil was burnt, leaving them in total darkness.

The water was up to their knees now, though the port hatch had gone under and the water was not coming in so fast, as the starboard hatch was only open a few inches.

They were trapped.

Rogers' immediate thought was of the bitter irony of the situation. Here he was, a fit and able man, imprisoned in a steel shell, breathing air, but unable to get out to the light above. He started to grope about for the hatch.

Commander Evans looked down and saw below his feet water coming in through the square hatch in the centre of the engine-room which is underneath the torpedo tubes on the upper deck and normally open a foot or so. Then a splash of water hit him in the face. He realised that the ship must be on her beam ends or even further over. He was aware that the movement of the ship had ceased. Everything was quite still and quiet and dark. The ship was floating completely upside down.

'Where's that bloody hatch?' shouted Rogers.

'I don't know. I can't find it!' yelled the E.R.A.

Somebody touched Commander Evans' elbow.

'Who's that?' he said.

'It's Rogers, sir,' said the stoker. 'Let's get out of here.'

'Well, there's your way out,' said the Commander quietly, pointing down at the hatch. 'Out you go, all of you.'

They looked down at the big, pale-green disc beneath their feet. The ship had capsized so fast that the air inside the engine-room had been trapped, forming an air lock so that the sea had flooded the compartment to a depth of only about four feet above what was originally the upper deck but which was now the bottom. The pale-green disc that they saw was the light shining through the circular hatch and the few feet of water above it.

Rogers lowered himself down until he felt the rim of the hatch, then pulled himself through feet first. When his head was down and clear of the hatch, he began to swim horizontally, with the ship above him, until he thought he was near the ship's side, then struck out for the surface. But he had misjudged the distance and found himself tangled up in the guardrails and the davits of the motor-cutter. For a moment he gave way to wild panic. He opened his mouth to scream, and gulped in salt water. Then he burst free and shot to the surface into the blinding white light, gasping in lungfuls of air, coughing, choking, spluttering, laughing and crying, all at the same time.

'Oh God! Oh God!' he cried out. 'They'll never get me now,' and began to laugh hysterically. Near him two men gave him a dirty look and started to swim away from him, thinking the shock had driven him mad. Then a head bobbed up a yard or two away. It was the E.R.A.

'O.K., Stokes?' he gasped.

'O.K. How's yourself?' said Rogers.

Another head bobbed up between them. It was Commander Evans.

He had waited until the last man had jumped through the hatch, then shouted, 'Is anybody else here?' The echo came back at him from the hollow shell arched above his head. He waited another moment, then, when there was no answer, threw off his tin hat and jumped through the hole. He sank down a short distance in the water. As he came up he wondered whether he would come up below the ship and drown underneath the upper deck or the torpedo tubes. Then his head hit something. It was the wire jackstay of the life-line along the upper deck. Then suddenly he rose into the sunlight and saw that he was several yards clear of the ship's side. He saw Rogers.

'You all right, Rogers?' he asked.

'Yes, sir, thanks,' spluttered the stoker.

'Good, then we'd better get away from the ship in case she goes,' he said.

They swam away, and when they thought they were far enough stopped and looked back at the ship, treading water.

The *Kelly* was floating capsized, with the whole length of the keel, from stem to stern, showing. Her screws were turning in the air still and several men still clung on to her keel. All around the ship the sea was dotted with heads, where men struggled, choking and groaning, in the black oil-fuel that by then had come out from the ship's tanks.

Rocky Wilkins struggled hard towards safety, away from the suction of the ship, which would pull him down and drown him if he were too close when she sank. He had been washed off the pom-pom. One minute he had his eye to the gunsight, the next he was in the water. He thought, 'Blimey, I'm going to get wet.' The ship was still making speed through the water and the sea was as hard as a brick wall. When he came up, the first man he saw was the Signals Officer. Rocky hung on to the officer's big American lifebelt until he managed to get hold of a beer crate that floated past and transferred himself to that. As he did so he passed a man lying on his back, his face black with oil fuel. It was the P.T.I.

'Clubs, are you all right?' asked Rocky hoarsely.

'I'm all right,' said the P.T.I. softly. Then his lips moved again.

'Ave Maria,' he whispered, looked upwards towards the light, and died.

Rocky had swallowed a lot of oil by now and was nearly exhausted. He was a bad swimmer and had reached his limit. The Frist Lieutenant saw he was in trouble. Swimming across, Lord Beresford dragged him over to the smashed Carley float which was all they had to hang on to. Rocky was clinging to the raft, when he saw his young oppo, whom he had sent below for some chocolate only a few minutes before.

'Here's your nutty, Wings,' whispered the boy.

Rocky lifted his head to thank him and saw that he was dead.

A man swam up to the raft.

'Old Tusky's gone,' he said. 'I saw him get drawn into the screws.'

Rocky looked around him, trying to recognise faces. He saw Lofty Howarth and Ted West. Then Lord Mountbatten swam up to the float, pulling a man behind him.

Between them the Captain and the First Lieutenant saved many men that day. Time and again they swam out to a man badly burned and hardly alive or gasping his heart out and about to drown, to bear him up and carry him back to the raft.

When he had done all that a human being could to help his shocked, sick and wounded shipmates, Captain Mountbatten swam back to the Carley float and looked across at the long black shape that was all that was left of the *Kelly*. She seemed about to go.

'Give her a cheer, lads,' he said. They raised a ragged burst of cheering as the ship tilted, then slowly sank.

Where the *Kelly* had been there was nothing. The sea had her now. Exhausted, sickened, hurt, the survivors thought of the many dear friends and messmates who had gone with her, down to the silence of green fathoms that would be their grave.

'Come on, lads,' said the Captain, 'let's have a song,' and himself started up 'Roll out the barrel'.

They sang, where they could, their throats burned raw with oil fuel, their strength nearly gone.

Roll out the barrel, let's have a barrel of fun,
Roll out the barrel, we've got the blues on the run.

They sang, coughing and choking over the words so often sung lustily in the warmth of the messdecks.

It was then that the Germans came back. They were not satisfied with sinking the *Kelly* and killing most of her men, so they came down low and machine-gunned the helpless survivors in the water.

'Bastards don't like the tune,' said one man.

'All right, we'll give 'em another then,' said Rocky, and started to sing. A few more joined in and they sang at the Stukas as they came down:

We're poor little lambs who have gone astray, baa,
baa, baa,
Little black sheep that have gone astray, baa, baa,
baa,
Gentlemen matelots all are we, doomed from here to
eternity,
God have mercy on such as we...

Rocky broke down coughing and the song died away.

Rogers trod water despairingly. By now the exhilaration of his miraculous escape had worn off. His lifebelt was leaking and he was too weak now to blow it up. He felt he would never see land again.

Then they heard gunfire and saw smoke on the horizon. Presently a ship came into sight, a destroyer, making all speed towards them. It was the *Kipling*.

Her steering gear repaired, she had come up just as the attack began and had immediately made two signals; the first:

From *Kipling*. To C.S.7. Dive-bombers attacking *Kelly* and *Kashmir*;

then, a few minutes later:

Kelly and *Kashmir* both sunk.

Half an hour later Captain Mountbatten was able to send the following signal to the Flag Officer, 7th Cruiser Squadron:

H.M.S. *Kipling* is still picking up survivors. Are you sending help?

When she came on the scene she made immediately for the survivors and began to lower her whaler, besides throwing all her spare rafts and any floatable material over the side for the exhausted men to cling on to.

The whaler pulled up near Rogers.

'Are you all right?' yelled the coxswain.

'Yes, but my lifebelt is leaking!' shouted Gordon feebly.

'Just hang on for a minute, lad!' shouted the other. 'There's a couple of wounded chaps here. I'll pick them up, take them back to the ship, then come back for you.'

A short time afterwards the whaler returned and Rogers, now barely conscious, was dragged over the side. He flopped into the bottom of the boat and knew no more until he felt a bump, looked up and saw that they were alongside the *Kipling*. Scrambling nets hung down from the ship's side. Rogers was much too weak to climb, but, between them, willing hands in the boat and on the deck above pulled, pushed and dragged him aboard. Gordon lay where they dropped him, thankful to feel the hard iron deck beneath him. Presently an officer came up and, supporting his head, tipped a glass of whisky down his throat. He felt the life returning as the warm spirit surged through his body.

In this way most of the surviving *Kelly* and *Kashmir* men were picked up, sick, hurt and exhausted, from the filthy black oil and wreckage. All the time the Germans came low, bombing and machine-gunning both rescuers and rescued, and several men were killed in the water.

Mountbatten, as Captain (D), had naturally taken charge of the operations aboard the *Kipling.* Seeing that every time the *Kipling* stopped beside one of the *Kashmir*'s Carley rafts the German dive-bombers attacked her and forced her to go ahead again, he ordered Lieutenant-Commander St Clair-Ford to lower his fast motor-boat with the idea that this boat could go round collecting people from the rafts and then dash quickly alongside the *Kipling* while she was stopped between attacks.

The motor-boat was lowered into the water, but she had no quick-release gear, so the crew had to unshackle the falls. At this precise moment another dive-bomber came in and St Clair-Ford warned Mountbatten that he was going ahead at full speed. Mountbatten yelled from the bridge:

'We are going ahead. Cut the boat's falls.'

Instead of cutting the after falls first, in the heat and confusion of the moment someone cut the foremost falls. As the *Kipling* started to gather way the bows of the boat turned outwards and she started to capsize. Mountbatten yelled:

'You bloody fools, cut the after falls!'

Immediately Lord Beresford, who had been among the last to be saved, and the First Lieutenant of the *Kipling*, Lieutenant Bush, leapt to the after falls to try and cut them free, but as the ship increased speed the terrible force dragged the davit out of its socket, taking both Beresford and Bush with it. In this desperate smash both men were killed.

Mountbatten then had to decide whether to stay and pick up the rest of the *Kashmir*'s ship's company or to make for Alexandria with all the *Kelly*'s survivors and about half of the *Kashmir's*. This was a decision which only he could make, in which no one could help him. He gave the order to remain and pick up the rest of the *Kashmir's* men.

They adopted a sort of tip-and-run procedure. The ship would dash in, pick up a few men, then withdraw again before the bombers could concentrate too heavily on them. Eventually, however, the attacks grew too hot for safety, and, having satisfied himself that all survivors had been rescued, Captain (D) gave the order to make for Alexandria. What was thought to be the empty whaler was left behind in the water. It was only some time afterwards that Mountbatten was told that one man had been seen standing up in the boat and saluting as the *Kipling* steamed away.

They still had four hundred miles to go.

To make things worse, the *Kipling*, in picking up some of the survivors, had come in too close and hit the submerged wreck of the *Kelly*, which was still floating at the time. The collision tore a great gash down her side, which slowed her down to twenty knots and released a stream of oil. All the bombers had to do after that was to follow the oil.

So she limped homewards, with a heavy list to port and most of her lower decks sealed off. The bombers attacked ceaselessly, setting up a wall of white water around the ship, which shuddered continuously from near misses. But they were not hit. Some put it down to a miracle, others to the great skill of Commander Ford in anticipating the direction of the enemy attacks and manoeuvring his ship to dodge the bombs.

In all, they beat off some forty attacks that morning until they were at last out of range of the enemy. Then the survivors settled down to make themselves as comfortable as possible. Rogers still had on his overalls, stokehold boots and socks, all soaked with oil-fuel. Rocky Wilkins had discarded his overalls and had dressed himself in a set of feminine scanties which had been used as cleaning rags on the guns. No one took any notice of him and he was past caring. There was only one thought in his head – he was alive.

As the ship limped home the Captain went round with a notebook and pencil, taking down messages for the next-of-kin of the most seriously injured men. In many cases he was unable to recognise men he knew quite well, so badly were they burned and so thickly covered with oil fuel. In some cases he had to read their names off their identity discs.

Many men died on that voyage. Some only lasted a minute or two after they had been picked up from the water. Others, knowing they had only a short time to live, lay quietly until their end came, then passed away without a word.

Before the ship reached Alexandria her fuel ran out and she lay still in the water. But before long the *Protector* came up in response to a signal and replenished her tanks.

Next morning they sighted Egypt. Happily they stared at the sand and palm trees along the coast, and at the white buildings of Alexandria gleaming in the distance. Then Commander Ford addressed them.

'The Fleet has heard of your magnificent action,' he said, 'and of all the trials you have undergone. They are waiting there in Alexandria to welcome you into harbour. As we go through the lock-gates they will be assembled on the upper decks of their ships, waiting to give you a rousing welcome.'

And so it was. About an hour later the survivors were lined up on either side of the *Kipling*'s upper deck. They were a scarecrow bunch now, clothed in rags and still dirty from the oil fuel. Those who could not stand raised themselves on their elbows, or simply listened as the tremendous roar of cheering echoed across the harbour – a long, heart-felt, continuous cheer that lasted until the ship came alongside, a cheer that said what no words could ever say for the little group of tired, shocked and wounded men who stood on the tilting deck so silently, thinking of the friends they had lost and the brave ship that now lay shattered at the bottom of the sea.

They finally tied up alongside No. 46 shed. Stretchers and ambulances were waiting for the wounded, and the others were taken aboard the repair ship the *Resource*, where they had a hot meal, a bath, and were issued with cigarettes and chocolate.

The *Kipling*'s boat took Mountbatten and several of the *Kelly*'s officers to the base. There they were met by a midshipman from the *Valiant*. It was his nephew, Prince Philip, who laughed sympathetically on seeing his uncle's face, blackened with oil fuel, and said, 'You look like a nigger minstrel.'

Rogers did not feel like getting into his oil-soaked overalls again, so he did the best he could with a small and rather ancient towel that he managed to borrow from someone on the *Resource*. In this abbreviated and decrepit bit of cloth he gave a half-hearted impersonation of a hula-hula girl. Another man borrowed two handkerchiefs, knotted them together, and created what must have been the first Bikini swimsuit.

When they went into No. 46 shed they found that fresh clothing was in short supply. Rogers was given one suit of underwear, a pair of tropical shorts and a tropical shirt, a pair of white stockings and white tropical shoes. There were no caps, so everyone was issued with a pith helmet. In this music-hall costume they were then taken off in buses to the Fleet Air Arm station at Dhekeila. Here they were put into tents, where they had their first full night's sleep for some weeks. The following afternoon they were each given a pound and allowed shore leave in Alexandria. A pound's-worth of beer will do a lot towards retrieving a man's spirits, and these men had a heavy sorrow to drown.

Then, on the following day, Mountbatten came and spoke to them. He said:

'I have come to say goodbye to the few of you who are left. We have had so many talks, but this is our last. I have always tried to crack a joke or two before, and you have all been friendly and laughed at them. But today I am afraid I have run out of jokes, and I don't suppose any of us feel much like laughing. The *Kelly* has been in one scrap after another, but even when we have had men killed the majority survived and brought the old ship back. Now she lies in fifteen hundred fathoms and with her more than half our shipmates. If they had to die, what a grand way to go, for now they all lie together with the ship we loved, and they are in very good company. We have lost her, but they are still with her. There may be less than half the *Kelly* left, but I feel that each of us will take up the battle with even stronger heart. Each of us knows twice as much about fighting, and each of us has twice as good a reason to fight. You will all be sent to replace men who have been killed in other ships, and the next time you are in action remember the *Kelly*. As you ram each shell home into the gun, shout, "*Kelly*!" and so her spirit will go on inspiring us until victory is won. I should like to add that there isn't one of you I wouldn't be proud and honoured to serve with again. Goodbye, good luck, and thank you all from the bottom of my heart.'

CHAPTER X

EPILOGUE IN THE DESERT

It was the end of a story – and the beginning of another. Like the *Courageous* and the *Rawalpindi*, the *Gloucester*, the *Fiji* and many other fine ships, the *Kelly* had stood the shock of the first great German attacks and had been sacrificed.

But the sacrifice was not in vain.

Two military defeats we had suffered, and survived. First, Dunkirk. Then Crete, the Dunkirk of the middle war.

Defeat and withdrawal in Greece and Crete had been almost inevitable. Our strength was pitifully small and, most decisive of all, we had next to no air power. The Luftwaffe was able to do what it would, unopposed.

But out of defeat we snatched a victory. It was a Pyrrhic one, and cold comfort at the time, but it bore fruit later. We could not hope to stop the German advance, but we might be able to damage it and slow it down. And so we did. In taking Crete the German army suffered heavy casualties. Prevented by the Mediterranean Fleet from landing by sea, their airborne forces were severely mauled by the Commonwealth troops and naval units defending the island and, thanks again to the Navy, they never got any farther.

From now on, after Crete, it was 'Hold on' in the West. The limit had been reached, the thin line we were determined not to cross. For months after Crete there were relatively minor reverses to be suffered, lesser victories to be won. But between our Dunkirks and our D-days the Germans could move us no farther. They were down to the rock.

Final victory is no isolated event, no sudden blessing. It is the sum of a long resistance, a result of the capacity and the will to win. Our two great material retreats were, for the spirit, advances. Dunkirk roused us, hit us at home where the nation's courage lay in restless unease, and after Dunkirk, Crete advanced our awakening still further. The lion stirred then, and awoke. Slowly it stretched its paws and sprang its claws out – new ships, planes, tanks and men.

We had survived to fight again, after suffering the worst that a berserk enemy could do to us.

That we had survived at all, however, we owed to the small advance-guard who had stood the first shock, the New Contemptibles of Wavell's army, the Few of the Battle of Britain, and the tired, battered but undefeated ships and men of the shoe-string navy, built and mobilised at the last minute, but just in time.

They still kept the seas, but they had suffered heavily. For the blindness and ineptitude of the pre-war years, wishful years of disarmament and rose-tinted pacifism, they had paid in splendid ships sunk and fine men killed before their time.

Yes, the shoe-string navy had suffered in its triumphant battle for our freedom. What was left? A reduced force of men and ships.

A reduced force – fifty men in a camp on the edge of a desert.

Here the men of the *Kelly* were given time to recover. They had no duties but were allowed to do what they pleased. For the most part they simply rested and bathed, bathed and rested, and felt they could never have enough of it. The slow time of the desert helped to heal their shocked minds; the space and silence of the sky gave them calm.

And gradually they began to feel restored to health. Some the ordeal had matured, had given wisdom which might otherwise never have come their way. A few, like Gordon Rogers, emerged from their suffering with the feeling that nothing more could harm them, the feeling which flashed upon Roger's mind when he rose up from the dying ship and said, 'They'll never get me now.'

This hard-won ripeness shone obliquely through the Captain's words of farewell, like a rainbow seen through clear water, when he said, 'I feel that each of us will take up the battle with stronger heart.'

They did take up the battle, and with stronger heart, in new ships and in new ways of life. They never forgot the *Kelly* and that last grim battle, and somehow they were better men for it.

Some time after the *Kelly* had gone Lord Beresford's body was washed up on the North African coast near Sollum, and buried there. Rocky Wilkins and other survivors went to see the grave and to pay their respects. And far from the burning sands of Africa, up in Hebburn-on-Tyne, the grave of those men who died in the cold North Sea is still freshly kept and tended by the Tynesiders.

Even today the men of the *Kelly* keep together. Each year they hold a reunion, which is attended by all those ex-*Kelly* officers and men who are not too far afield to make the journey to London.

CHRONOLOGICAL NOTE

1937	April	2nd	– Contract signed for 'No. 615'.
	August	26th	– Keel laid.
1938	October	25th	– The *Kelly* launched.
1939	August	23rd	– The *Kelly* commissioned.
	September	3rd	– War declared.
	"	4th	– U-boat sunk by the *Kelly* and the *Acheron*.
	"	12th	– The *Kelly* brings Duke and Duchess of Windsor to England from Le Havre.
	"	17th	– The *Courageous* sunk.
	October	14th	– Second U-boat sunk.
1940	April	29th	– Evacuation of Namsos began.
	May	9th	– The *Kelly* torpedoed.
1941	May	21st	– Invasion of Crete.
	"	23rd	– The *Kelly* sunk by dive-bombers.

GLOSSARY OF NAVAL TERMS

A.A.3: Anti-aircraft rating, third class.

Aggie Weston's: Sailor's abbrevation for the hostels founded by Dame Agnes Weston.

All-night-in: A watchkeeping term. The system of watches is so arranged that a man may count on one uninterrupted night's sleep every few days.

Ambit: A potent Maltese drink.

Andrew: Slang for the Royal Navy, derived from Andrew Miller, a nineteenth-century naval contractor.

Asdic: Submarine detection apparatus.

Bangers: Sausages.

Barrack stanchion: One who props up the barracks, i.e. a sailor who has found simultaneously a soft job in R.N.B. and a method of avoiding a draft to sea.

Buffer: Chief Boatswain's Mate – senior chief or petty officer of the Seaman Branch in H.M. ships.

Bull-ring: Large eye at the stem of a destroyer for mooring purposes.

Bunch of bastards: A slovenly arrangement, a tangle.

Burn: To smoke a cigarette.

Buzz: Rumour.

Captain (D): Service abbreviation for Captain (Destroyers), the senior officer in command of a flotilla.

Casual: A 'casual' payment, made at a time other than the normal fortnightly pay-day. Very hard to come by.

Chief Yeoman: Chief Yeoman of Signals, the senior petty officer of the Signals Branch.

Chokka-block: Fed up, browned or cheesed off. Sometimes 'two-blocks' or simply 'chokka'.

Clear lower deck: An order mustering the entire ship's company.

Deckhead: Ceiling.

Defaulters: Parade of offenders against King's Regulations and Admiralty Instructions.

Dghaisa: Maltese gondola.

Dockyard mateys: Dockyard workmen. Often abused, sometimes unjustly.

Eye-shooting: Gunnery term referring to the method of sighting a light anti-aircraft gun.

Flash up: To get steam up.

Flats: Open spaces between decks; for example, tiller flat, wardroom flat, sick-bay flat.

Friday while: A long weekend.

Gash: Rubbish.

Geordie: A Tynesider.

Gestapo: The barrack guard at Royal Naval Barracks, Chatham. Often applied generally to the Regulating Branch, the Navy's police force.

G.I.: Gunnery Instructor – senior petty officer of the Gunnery Branch.

Green rub: A raw deal, unfair treatment.

Guz: Royal Naval Barracks, Devonport.

Hammock net: Stowage space for hammocks.

Heads: Lavatories.

Heaving lines: Light lines thrown from ship to shore when coming alongside, their inboard ends attached to the ship's mooring wires.

Hogwash: The sea.

Hook: Anchor.

Hookie: A leading seaman, derived from the badge he wears on his arm.

Jimmy: 'Jimmy-the-One' – the First Lieutenant.

Jose: Sailor's name for a Maltese.

Killick: Leading seaman.

Ky: Cocoa.

Lash up and stow: Lash up your hammock and stow it away!

Last dog: Last dog watch, the watch from six to eight p.m.

Neaters: Neat rum.

No-badge A.B.s: Men rated able seamen before having qualified for long-service and good-conduct badges. A term of derision.

O.D.: Ordinary seaman. A term of contempt.

Oppo: Opposite number, particular chum.

Part of ship: General duties in a ship.

Party: Girl-friend.

Ping: Sound made by the Asdic when a contact has been made with a submerged object.

Pom-pom: Multiple-barrelled, short-range anti-aircraft gun.

Pusser's: Purser's' – official stores.

Q.E.: The battleship *Queen Elizabeth.*

Rabbits: Articles of bargaining value to be smuggled ashore.

Ready-use ammunition: Ammunition kept in racks on the gun platform for immediate use in an emergency.

Rattle: The First Lieutenant's Report of defaulters.
Rubber: A loan.
Run ashore: Shore Leave.
Sardines: Torpedoes.
Scouse: A native of Liverpool.
Sea lawyers: Lower-deck agitators.
Shower: Rabble.
Seen off. Swindled.
Sick-bay tiffy: Sick-berth attendant.
Sippers: The present of sips from another man's daily issue of rum.
Skate: Ne'er-do-well.
Slops: The slop chest or naval stores.
Smoke: London.
Snake Pit: A place of entertainment, at one time out of bounds to naval personnel.
Sprog: Young rookie.
Stand-easy: Break at mid-morning and afternoon.
Station keeping: Preserving a prescribed position relative to other ships in company.
Still: A pipe or bugle call.
Stripey: An ancient seaman, usually the possessor of three good conduct 'stripes'.
Sweeper: Cleaner.
Swinging round the buoy: Spending much time in harbour.
Temperance rating: A shipboard teetotaller, receiving threepence per day in lieu of his issue of rum or 'grog' and officially marked 'T'. Those drawing their issue are marked 'G' and those under age (under twenty) 'U.A.'.
Ticklers: Cigarettes rolled by hand using officially issued tobacco.
Tiddley: Smart.
Tiddley oggies: Cornish pasties.
Tombola: Naval name for Housey-housey, a game with numbers.

Tot: Measure of rum.
Up homers: In the bosom, usually, of one's party's family. (v. 'party').
Up the line: On leave.
Wings: Term of affection for a chum.

PQ17 – CONVOY TO HELL

by Paul Lund and Harry Ludlam

In June, 1942, Convoy PQ17, consisting of thirty-five merchant ships, set out for Russia with an escort of cruisers and destroyers. They had a reasonable chance of success until the order came to 'Scatter!'

What followed represents one of the most terrible and tragic blunders of the Second World War.

Authors Ludlam and Lund give a first hand account of the horror and despair that faced the men left to the mercy of a cruel enemy. From thousands of sources and recollections they have built up an unforgettable picture of what it was like to be in PQ17 – and survive . . .

NEW ENGLISH LIBRARY